# The Young Road Traveller's Handbook

# The Young Road Traveller's Handbook

## Peter Eldin

Hamlyn
London·New York·Sydney·Toronto

## Acknowledgements

I would like to express my sincere thanks to all those who have helped in the preparation of this book, particularly Leigh Jones. Many people have been most kind in answering my queries and sorting out some of the problems and I am grateful to them for their help. Thank you also to the manufacturers, associations, and individuals who have provided information and illustrative material.

Illustrations by David Eaton, Industrial Art Studio St. Ives, Bob Mathias, Stuart Perry, John Shackell, Robin Wade Design Associates, Gerald Witcomb, Michael Youens.

Aberdeen City District Council 172; Beamish North of England Open Air Museum, Stanley, 83; Alan Beaumont, Lowestoft 98, 99 left and right; John Bethell, St Albans 40, 41 left, 82; British Tourist Authority, London 21, 37 top, 41 right, 42–43, 77 top, 78, 80, 92; British Transport Films, London 37 bottom; A. N. Browne, London 15 bottom; Central Office of Information, London 47; W. F. Davidson, Penrith 2–3, 19, 72 top and bottom left, 72–73, 76, 77 bottom, 94, 96, 163 top; Hamlyn Group – John Howard 55; H. Hodson, London 6–7; M. Hodson, London 165; Jarrold and Sons Ltd, Norwich 90; National Museum of Wales (Welsh Folk Museum), St Fagans 85; National Trust, London 101; Northern Ireland Tourist Board, Belfast 171; Charles Pocklington, London 45; G. R. Roberts, Nelson 15 top left and top right; Spectrum Colour Library, London 37 centre; R. Thomlinson, Carlisle 173.

The illustrations on pages 30–32, 34–36, 46, and 186/187 are reproduced with permission of the Controller of Her Majesty's Stationery Office.

Published 1979 by
The Hamlyn Publishing Group Limited
London · New York · Sydney · Toronto
Astronaut House, Feltham, Middlesex, England.
© Copyright The Hamlyn Publishing Group Limited 1979

ISBN 0 600 39535 9

Printed in Italy by New Interlitho

# Contents

# Introduction

What do you do on long road journeys when you have read all your books and comics and eaten all the sweets? Do you look out of the car window for a while only to find there is little of interest so you sink into a gloomy silence for the rest of the trip? If you find this is the case then this book should be of use to you. In writing this book I have tried to provide you with an introduction to some of the fascinating things you can investigate during a journey, together with a wealth of information regarding things you will see whilst on the road. I have not been able to deal with each subject exhaustively for to do so would require a book many times the size of this one. I hope, however, that you will find sufficient information to whet your appetite and encourage you to investigate the subjects further. It is much more exciting to make your own discoveries than to read about them. So make the most of your eyes, look around at the things you pass on your journey, question their purpose or origins, and you will gradually realise that no road journey, no matter how long it may be, is a boring affair.

*Have a good trip*

Peter Eldin

6

# Preparing for the Journey

This book will help you make the most of your journeys by road. On the following pages you will find lots of things that you can do, and lots of things you can look out for whilst travelling, especially on long journeys. Before you make a trip by road, there are several simple ways in which you can make the journey more enjoyable.

The first, and most important consideration, is advance preparation. Put together everything you will need several days before your journey, so that you avoid the usual last minute rush. It is a good idea to write out a list of the things you will need on route and tick each item off the list as you put it into the bag or case that you intend to carry with you.

## What to take with you

Some of the items you should consider putting on your list are:

*plenty of comics and magazines*
*sweets ( boiled are best)*
*pencils*
*crayons*
*plenty of drawing or writing paper*
*a copy of the Highway Code*

You could also take a travelling chess set, a book or two, a pack of cards and a transistor radio. If you plan to play any word games a small dictionary will be found useful in settling any disputes that may arise. A cassette tape recorder and plenty of tapes will also help to make the journey go that much quicker, and do not forget that there are plenty of

Some things to take on the journey.

excellent story tapes on the market.

All of these items can be accommodated in a carrier bag, but a better solution is to use a small case, as this will provide a useful 'table top' when one is required for a game, for writing, or for drawing. If you have not got a case, then an old tray, or a large, firm book will do just as well. A separate bag should be taken for the rubbish, the sweet papers, empty cans, and so on that one invariably accumulates on a long journey. A plastic bag is best for this purpose as it can easily be dumped into the nearest waste-paper bin when you reach your destination.

Before the start of your journey make a note of the mileage reading on the odometer. Take another reading when you reach your destination and you will be able to calculate the distance covered. If you also make a note of the time at the start and finish of the journey you will also be able to calculate the average speed attained by dividing the number of miles by the time taken.

You will find that the journey will be more interesting if you follow it on a map. Try working out the route beforehand and discuss the best way to go with the driver if possible. See what rivers you are likely to cross and then follow their routes from source to sea. Make a note of any towns you will travel through. Perhaps, if you look at the route several days in advance, you can find out whether or not each town is famous for any particular reason, and can look out for any interesting buildings or land marks.

Even if you do not have a chance to prepare in advance for your journey you can make it interesting for yourself by just keeping your eyes and mind open. Some clues as to the many and varied things you can see on your journey are given on the pages that follow. But the main emphasis remains upon your own observations, for to include everything that you are likely to see would necessitate a book several times the size of this one. The British Isles are full of interesting, even amazing and curious things but the best way to find them is through your own investigations.

## Planning the route

Before starting any journey you must plan out the route you are going to take. When doing this you must take into consideration what type of journey you wish to have. Do you want to reach your destination quickly and without fuss or would you rather take your time, go through the most pleasant scenery, and do some sightseeing on the way? Upon your answer will depend what route you eventually take. It should also be remembered when planning any road journey that the shortest route is not necessarily the quickest way to reach your destination. With a car journey, for example, it will usually be a lot faster to go along a motorway even though it does not go to the exact point that you wish. A relatively fast journey along the motorway could well compensate for any small delay caused by the fact that you have gone slightly out of your way.

When planning the route keep a watchful eye open for anything that may hamper your progress. If you are in a hurry you will not choose a route that requires travelling on a ferry for there is bound to be some delay at the boarding point. Also, if in a hurry, it is worthwhile avoiding large towns if this is possible as they are another regular cause of hold ups.

To find out the total distance of the journey you are about to take it is useful to use an opisometer. This is a small wheeled device that is run along the route on the map. As the opisometer runs over the map it measures the distance that it has travelled. When you reach the end of the planned route all you have to do is look at the reading on the opisometer and, using the scale given for the particular map, convert the reading of inches (or centimetres) into the correct number of miles or kilometres.

If you want to measure the distance and you do not wish to buy an opisometer you can do exactly the same thing with a length of cotton. Carefully lay the cotton on the map along the route that you wish to take. When you get to journey's end simply measure the

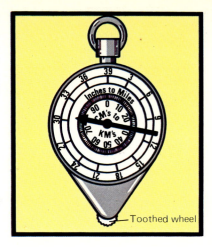

*Above:* An opisometer for measuring distances on a map. *Right:* A section of a map of the Cardiff area.

© John Bartholomew & Son Ltd.

piece of cotton and convert the inches or centimetres into miles or kilometres.

## How to read a map

You will gain a great deal of additional pleasure from your travels on the road if you learn how to read maps. A map does not only tell you the quickest way of getting from one place to another, it also provides a great deal of information about the area through which you are travelling.

A map is a pictorial representation of the country or part of it drawn to a scaled-down size. Somewhere on every map you will find a reference to the particular scale that

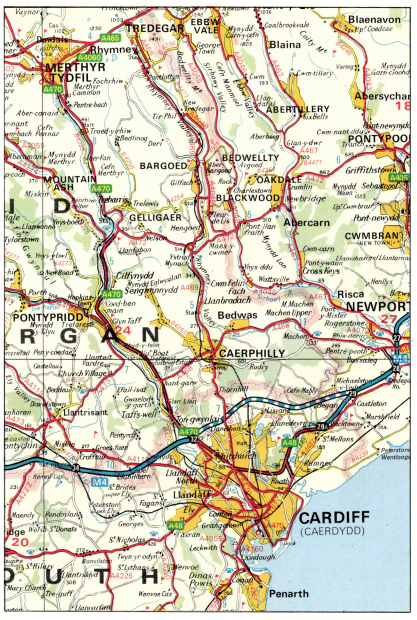

nas been used. This is indicated in one of three ways:

(1) in words, such as *one inch equals five miles*.

(2) by a representative fraction such as $\frac{1}{316800}$ (or 1:316,800). This indicates that each inch (2·54 cm) on the map represents 316,800 inches (804,672 cm) in actual fact. If you care to work this out you will find that 316,800 inches are equal to 5 miles (8 kilometres) so that the map is in fact drawn to the same scale as in the first example.

(3) with a line marked with the units represented as shown here:

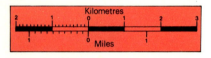

Conventional symbols used on maps.

## Map symbols

The first thing to do when looking at a map is to familiarise yourself with the symbols used. They will tell you a great deal about the area at which you are looking. At first sight the symbols are perhaps a little confusing but with a little practice you will soon become familiar with most of them. The symbols shown here are like those used on Ordnance Survey maps. As a general rule most of the maps produced in Britain are derived from Ordnance Survey maps, and many of the symbols used are the same as well. Some map publishers, however, use their own symbols and conventions for certain items, so it is always useful to look at the section of the map called 'the legend', that gives the relevant details of the symbols used.

# Conventional signs

| | | | |
|---|---|---|---|
| | Main road | | Marsh |
| | Secondary road | | Cliff |
| | Minor road | | Wood |
| | Track | | Orchard |
| | Unfenced track | | Church with tower |
| | Path | | Church with spire |
| | Railway | | Triangulation pillar |
| | Bridge | 100 | Contours at 20m intervals |
| | Level crossing | ·148 | Spot heights |
| | Cutting | P | Post office |
| | Embankment | PH | Public house |
| | | T | Telephone call box |

## How to make a strip map

A particularly useful sort of map to use for any road journey is a strip map. It gives the traveller all the information needed, and at the same time cuts out any unnecessary information.

To make a strip map of your planned route simply draw a straight line and mark along it details of the roads you have to take, where you have to turn left or right, and the distances from place to place. There is no need to draw this map to scale, so it can be drawn on a small piece of paper. It is therefore easier to handle than a conventional map.

The drawing on this page shows a strip map for a journey from Prestatyn to Pwllheli. If you have a road map follow the route on it using the strip map as a guide.

## What's the weather going to be like?

It is useful to have some advance information regarding weather conditions, both along your route and at your ultimate destination. The weather can make a great deal of difference to any journey. Bad conditions, such as ice, fog or heavy rain, can be dangerous, and only journeys that are absolutely necessary should be made in such conditions. Good weather can help make a journey pleasant and less troublesome but it can also lead to problems, such as the car engine

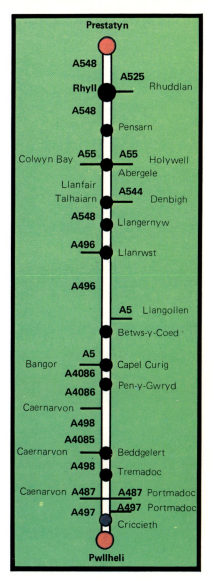

A strip map makes it easy to follow your route.

overheating in hot weather, and can affect a driver's visibility when the light is too bright.

The daily newspapers carry weather forecasts, and there are also regular forecasts on television and radio. It is also possible to find out the weather in particular areas by telephoning the local meteorological office, the telephone number of which will be found in the telephone directory for the area.

It is also possible to find out the local, national and continental weather conditions by telephoning or calling at one of the following weather centres:

*Glasgow*, Strathclyde, 118 Waterloo Street. Tel. 041 248 3451
*London*, 284/286, High Holborn. Tel. 01 836 4311
*Manchester*, Greater Manchester, 56 Royal Exchange. Tel. 061 832 6701
*Newcastle*, Tyne and Wear, 7th Floor, Newgate House, Newgate Street. Tel. Newcastle 26453
*Nottingham*, Nottinghamshire, Main Road, Watnall. Tel. Hucknall 3311
*Southampton*, Hampshire, 160 High Street, Below Bar. Tel. Southampton 28844

**Weather signs**

It is much more interesting, however, to try your own hand at weather forecasting. There are many ways of doing this. Many people rely on a piece of seaweed hung in the porch of a house. If the seaweed is dry and brittle the weather will remain dry, but if it is rubbery and feels damp to the touch then rain is indicated. A similar method is to watch a fir cone. The cone opens when rain is due and closes up when it is going to be sunny.

There are many signs in nature that can give indications of the weather to come. Here are some that you may like to check next time you are out: dead branches cracking in a wood – rain to come; red sky in the evening – fine weather; chimney smoke moving down before rising – rain later; larks flying high – fine and sunny; clouded yellow sunset – heavy rain and high wind; cows lying down – rain to come.

Red sky at night means a fine day tomorrow.

**Clouds**

A more reliable way of telling the weather to come is by looking at the clouds. Ten types of cloud are recognised by meteorologists but they are all formed as combinations or subdivisions of three basic types: **cirrus** – delicate, wispy clouds

Cirrus clouds form high in the sky.

Cumulus – often seen on a summer's day.

Stratus is a layer of grey cloud formed at a low level.

formed only at heights of over 8 kilometres (5 miles); **cumulus** – 'heap' clouds, thick and fluffy in appearance, formed between 490 and 6,100 metres (1,600 and 20,000 feet); and **stratus** – a sheet of layer cloud, grey in appearance, formed below 1,520 metres (5,000 feet).

Further description is sometimes provided by a prefix that indicates the height or the nature of the cloud. These prefixes are: cirro – high, formed at around 6,100 metres (20,000 feet); alto – middle height, formed at 4,270 metres (14,000 feet); strato – low, below 1,520 metres (5,000 feet); and nimbo – a rain cloud.

The ten types of cloud and the

weather conditions you can tell from them are as shown below.

A further indication of the weather to come is the speed at which the clouds are moving across the sky. If they are moving quickly it is a sure sign that wind and rain are on the way. When the clouds move only slowly the weather will probably remain fine. Clouds moving south when the wind is to the north is a sign of warmer weather.

| Name | Description | Weather |
| --- | --- | --- |
| Cirrus | hair-like and wispy | fine weather but rain is due if the clouds thicken. |
| Cirrocumulus | thick and fluffy | rain is on its way. |
| Cirrostratus | a thin white layer | bad weather to come. |
| Altocumulus | patches of small clouds | when positioned high they usually indicate good weather, if they are low then rain can be expected. |
| Altostratus | uniform grey sheet of cloud | rain, especially if changing to Nimbostratus |
| Stratocumulus | rolling bank of thick cloud | fine weather. |
| Stratus | pale grey in thin layers | if they clear in the morning fine weather is likely, but if they remain then rain can be forecast. |
| Nimbostratus. | dark grey layer at low level | rain or snow. |
| Cumulus | fluffy, like cotton wool | during the day an indication of continuing fine weather; seen early morning could indicate thunder; seen late evening means a fine day tomorrow. |
| Cumulonimbus | towering, dense and dark | heavy rain is due. |

# Sunshine

## Average Daily Sunshine (hours)

| | England, & Wales | Scotland | N. Ireland |
|---|---|---|---|
| January | 1·59 | 1·40 | 1·51 |
| February | 2·43 | 2·53 | 2·45 |
| March | 3·67 | 3·36 | 3·29 |
| April | 5·27 | 4·99 | 5·01 |
| May | 6·31 | 5·74 | 6·15 |
| June | 6·79 | 5·79 | 5·71 |
| July | 5·88 | 4·81 | 4·36 |
| August | 5·48 | 4·48 | 4·52 |
| September | 4·44 | 3·71 | 3·58 |
| October | 3·25 | 2·70 | 2·66 |
| November | 1·94 | 1·73 | 1·95 |
| December | 1·47 | 1·14 | 1·20 |

# Temperature

## Average Daily Temperature (°C at sea level)

| | England, & Wales | Scotland | N. Ireland |
|---|---|---|---|
| January | 4·0 | 3·5 | 4·0 |
| February | 4·2 | 3·7 | 4·3 |
| March | 6·2 | 5·4 | 6·2 |
| April | 8·8 | 7·5 | 8·2 |
| May | 11·6 | 9·9 | 10·8 |
| June | 14·7 | 12·7 | 13·5 |
| July | 16·3 | 14·1 | 14·7 |
| August | 16·1 | 14·0 | 14·6 |
| September | 14·3 | 12·5 | 13·0 |
| October | 11·2 | 9·9 | 10·4 |
| November | 7·2 | 6·3 | 6·7 |
| December | 5·1 | 4·6 | 5·0 |

# Rainfall

## Average Rainfall (centimetres)

| | England, & Wales | Scotland | N. Ireland |
|---|---|---|---|
| January | 9·2 | 15·4 | 10·9 |
| February | 6·6 | 10·6 | 7·6 |
| March | 5·7 | 8·9 | 6·6 |
| April | 6·0 | 8·8 | 6·7 |
| May | 6·3 | 8·7 | 7·2 |
| June | 5·5 | 8·7 | 7·1 |
| July | 7·9 | 11·4 | 9·6 |
| August | 8·1 | 12·2 | 10·2 |
| September | 7·6 | 12·8 | 9·6 |
| October | 9·2 | 15·8 | 11·1 |
| November | 9·5 | 14·3 | 10·4 |
| December | 8·8 | 14·3 | 11·1 |

To convert centigrade to fahrenheit first multiply by 9, then divide by 5, and then add 32. For example:

$$10·4°C = 51°F$$
$$10·4 \times 9 = 93·6$$
$$\div 5 = 18·72$$
$$+ 32 = 50·72$$

A rough conversion from centigrade to fahrenheit can be made by doubling the centigrade figure, and then adding 30.

| Force | 0 | 1 | 2 | 3 | 4 | 5 |
|---|---|---|---|---|---|---|
| Description | Calm | Light air | Light breeze | Gentle breeze | Moderate | Fresh |
| Effect | | | | | | |
| Weather symbol | | | | | | |

## Wind force

The force of the wind is measured according to the Beaufort Scale. This was devised by Sir Francis Beaufort in 1806 as a form of shorthand for sailors who had to record weather conditions in the ship's log. The scale ranges in force from zero to twelve as follows:

Force 0    Calm weather

Force 1    Smoke is moved by the wind but it is not strong enough to move a weather vane.

Force 2    Weather vanes begin to move and leaves rustle; wind felt on face.

Force 3    Leaves and small twigs in constant motion.

Force 4    Loose paper blows about and dust is raised.

Force 5    Ripples appear on expanses of water; small trees sway.

Force 6    Large branches sway; whistling heard in telegraph wires.

Force 7    Extremely blustery; whole trees sway; walking is difficult.

| 6 | 7 | 8 | 9 | 10 | 11 | 12 |
|---|---|---|---|---|---|---|
| Strong | Moderate gale | Gale | Strong gale | Whole gale | – | – |

*Above:* The Beaufort scale of wind strength.  *Below:* Windy weather ahead.

Force 8    Gale force; the wind is strong enough to break twigs off trees.

Force 9    Strong gale; slates can be dislodged from roofs.

Force 10    Whole gale; seldom occurs on land but when it does trees can be torn up by the roots.

Force 11    Causes great damage but, luckily, does not occur very often.

Force 12    Hurricane; occurs mainly in tropical areas.

# On the Road

## History of road building

Roads are essential to civilisation for they provide the vital links between one community and another. It is certain that even the ancient trackways of the British Isles were first developed for this very same reason – they provided a means of communication and trade between settlements.

At first the trackways would have consisted of nothing more than a cleared or beaten-down area of land. When man first started to use the horse for travelling from place to place the trackways would have become widened but, apart from the occasional clearing of bushes and undergrowth, no deliberate effort was made to create definite highways for the use of travellers. Traces of these ancient trackways can still be found in some parts of the country and sometimes more complete examples, such as the Harsoway which runs from Devon to Cornwall, still exist.

So trackways were established simply by continual use. Marker stones were erected every so often to let the traveller know that he was still on course. Gradually, as trade between communities increased, it became necessary to strengthen the trackways in certain places, for better and stronger roads were now required for the horse-drawn carts that were coming into use. Traces of these roads can still be found, the best-known being the Icknield Way, a prehistoric track in parts later built up as a Roman road, that ran from Avebury in Wiltshire to Hunstanton in Norfolk. Two other ancient tracks that you can find on modern maps are Ermine Street (which runs from London to Lincoln, with an extension to Scotland) and Fosse Way – which runs from Exeter to Lincoln.

The first real roads in Britain were created by the Romans who conquered these lands some two thousand years ago. The Romans built good roads so that their armies could move from one part of the country to another at speed. The shortest distance between any two points is a straight line, and the Romans built their roads straight, in accordance with this principle. To ensure that the road headed directly for the correct destination they employed men to light beacon fires at the high spots along the way, and the road builders followed these bonfires.

The four main groups of roads of the Roman period radiated from London. One ran to Silchester in Hampshire and then to the south-west of England; another went to Canterbury and the Kentish ports; the third went to the north-east,

20

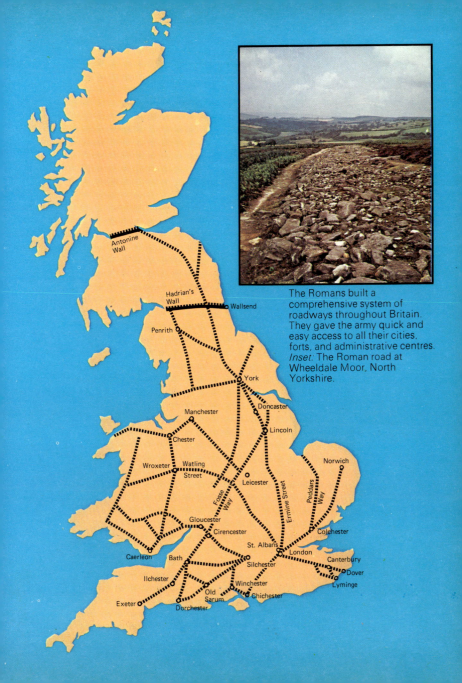

The Romans built a comprehensive system of roadways throughout Britain. They gave the army quick and easy access to all their cities, forts, and administrative centres. *Inset:* The Roman road at Wheeldale Moor, North Yorkshire.

Antonine Wall

Hadrian's Wall

Wallsend

Penrith

York

Manchester

Doncaster

Lincoln

Chester

Wroxeter

Watling Street

Norwich

Leicester

Fosse Way

Ermine Street

Peddars Way

Gloucester

Cirencester

Colchester

St. Albans

London

Caerleon

Bath

Canterbury

Silchester

Dover

Ilchester

Winchester

Lyminge

Exeter

Old Sarum

Chichester

Dorchester

through Colchester, and then to Lincoln and York; and the fourth ran through St Albans and on to Chester.

Many Roman roads still survive, the most notable being Watling Street, which runs from Dover to Chester. Much of the modern A5 follows the original route of Watling Street. The northern extension of Watling Street, known as De Vere Street, extended as far as Scotland. Part of it forms the present A68 but a great deal is now hidden under farmland and buildings. It can, however, still be followed over much of its route and some of it, particularly in Roxburghshire, has been extensively signposted.

Just like the ancient Britons before them, the Romans used marker stones along the route. These stones were positioned every thousand paces along the road and it is from the use of these posts that our word 'mile' originated, for the Italian for a thousand is *mille*.

## After the Romans

When the Romans left these shores in 410 AD the system of the roads quickly fell into decline, became overgrown, and were largely forgotten. Over a thousand years later, in 1555, a highways act was passed in an attempt to repair and recover some of the excellent road systems that had existed. But by that time the skills of road building had been forgotten, and the act proved to be rather a failure.

Roads did not improve greatly until methods of transport were improved. With the advent of the stage coach in the seventeenth century it was becoming increasingly obvious that some system for

How a Roman road was constructed.

Large gravel    Limy gravel    Limestone slabs    Hard gravel    Stiff clay improvement had to be devised. The first of these was the Turnpike Act of 1663 which authorised the setting up of tollgates at which fees could be collected from road users, as a means of raising money for the upkeep of the roads. There was so much abuse of the system, however, that little was done to improve the roads.

It was not until the eighteenth century that any real effort was made to improve the road system of the British Isles. The incentive came as a result of the Jacobite Rebellion of 1715 when it became obvious that a better road system was needed if the British army was to be an effective defence force. In 1726 General Wade began building new roads across the Scottish Highlands and it was not long before the ancient art of road building was being rediscovered, and developed even further. Other road building

pioneers of this period included Thomas Telford, the famous engineer, and John Macadam, whose methods of road building are still used today. In fact, our modern word 'tarmac' is derived from the surname of this great man.

The advent of the motor car revolutionised the roads of Britain. As the car became available to more people it became necessary to vastly improve the existing network of roads. To aid in this reorganisation the Ministry of Transport was set up in 1919.

Dual carriageways were first built during the 1930s, and by 1950 there were some 200,000 miles of classified roads in Britain. Then came the era of the motorway – fast, wide roads linking the main centres of the country and built with the motor age firmly in mind. Five motorways were started in the 1950s. These

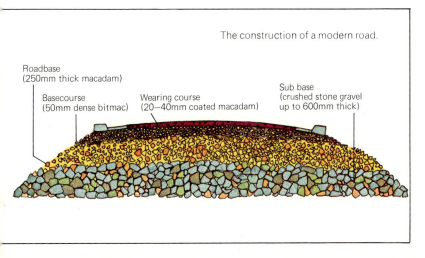

The construction of a modern road.

Roadbase
(250mm thick macadam)

Basecourse
(50mm dense bitmac)

Wearing course
(20–40mm coated macadam)

Sub base
(crushed stone gravel
up to 600mm thick)

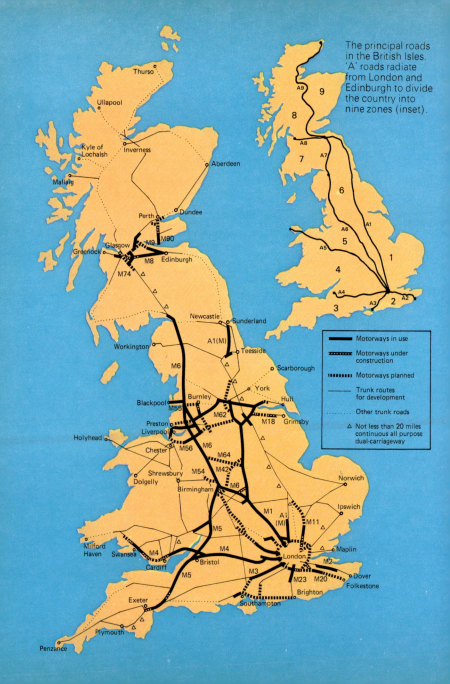

The principal roads
in the British Isles.
'A' roads radiate
from London and
Edinburgh to divide
the country into
nine zones (inset).

Thurso
Ullapool
Kyle of
Lochalsh
Inverness
Mallaig
Aberdeen
Perth
Dundee
M9 M90
Glasgow
Greenock
Edinburgh
M8
M74
Newcastle
Sunderland
A1(M)
Workington
Teesside
M6
Scarborough
York
Blackpool
Burnley
Hull
M55
M62
Preston
M18
Grimsby
Liverpool
Holyhead
Chester
M56
M6
M64
Shrewsbury
M54
M42
Dolgelly
M6
Birmingham
Norwich
M1
Ipswich
A1
(M)
M11
Milford
Haven
M4
M5
M4
Swansea
Cardiff
M4
Bristol
Maplin
London
M5
M3
M2
Exeter
M23
M20
Dover
Folkestone
Brighton
Southampton
Plymouth
Penzance

9
8
7
6
5
4
3
2
1
A9
A8
A7
A6
A5
A4
A3
A2
A1

Motorways in use
Motorways under
construction
Motorways planned
Trunk routes
for development
Other trunk roads
Not less than 20 miles
continuous all purpose
dual-carriageway

were the M1 from London to Yorkshire; the M2 from London to the Medway towns; the M4 from London to South Wales; the M5 from Birmingham to Bristol; and the M6 from Birmingham to Carlisle. The first to be opened was the initial section of the M6, the Preston By-pass, on the 5th December, 1958.

## How roads are classified

When you look at signposts you will see that in addition to the place name (and often the distance in miles) there is usually a letter and a number. The letter denotes the class of road, and each road in a particular class has its own number. There are, in fact, four different classes into which roads are placed. Three of these are allocated one of the letters A, B, or M (motorway). The fourth category does not have a letter and is not classified; these are minor roads.

The most important roads in Britain apart from motorways are allocated an A prefix. If you look carefully at a road map you will be able to see that mainland Britain is split up into nine different zones by the roads numbered A1 to A9. Six roads fan out from London like the spokes of a great wheel and three roads are centred on Edinburgh. The six roads from London are the A1, the Great North Road which goes all the way up to Edinburgh; the A2, which goes to Dover; the A3,

which goes down to Portsmouth; the A4 to Bath; the A5 to Holyhead; and lastly the A6, which leads to Carlisle. The three roads fanning out from Edinburgh are the A7, which runs south to Carlisle; the A8 to Gourock; and the A9 from Edinburgh to Inverness.

All the other roads are numbered with the first number allocated according to where the road starts. Thus, a road that starts somewhere in the zones bordered by the A4 and the A5 will start with the number 4; such as the A43 which runs from just north of Oxford up to Stamford. If you look at a map you will see that this road crosses over both the A5 and the A6, but it retains the number of the zone (4) in which it started.

The funds to pay for the upkeep of roads in the British Isles comes from the government and the local authorities through which the roads pass. The principal A roads, some-times called trunk routes, and the motorways are financed wholly by the government. For the less impor-tant A roads the government pays only threequarters of the cost of their upkeep. For B roads the government proportion is only half, the other half coming from the local authorities. All unclassified roads are the sole responsibility of the local authorities.

## Keep to the left

The rule of the road in the British

Isles is that you should always drive or ride on the left. In the rest of Europe the rule is exactly the opposite – you must keep to the right. In recent years there has been a great deal of discussion regarding the advantages and disadvantages of changing the British rule to conform to the rest of Europe, but so far no decision has been taken to change over.

It is not known for certain exactly why we drive on the left hand side of the road. Some authorities have suggested that it is a legacy from the days of medieval knights. Because the majority of people are right handed the knights always rode on the left side of a track so that their sword (right) hand was in the best position for defence or attack if another horseman passed by. If this is true it should naturally follow that the horsemen in the rest of Europe

would do the same thing and so road users on the Continent should now be driving on the left also.

Why are they different? The experts have a possible answer to this conundrum as well. Apparently it was the custom in warfare, for the same reason quoted above, to always attack from the left flank. Napoleon, however, decided to confuse his enemies by reversing this rule and attacking on the right flank. As this tactic proved successful he ordered that his troops should also keep to the right-hand side of the road. Eventually this rule was extended to include civilians of both France and the countries that Napoleon had conquered.

And so, Britain and Sweden were

Riding on the left came about because the soldier's sword arm (usually his right) was then in the best attacking position.

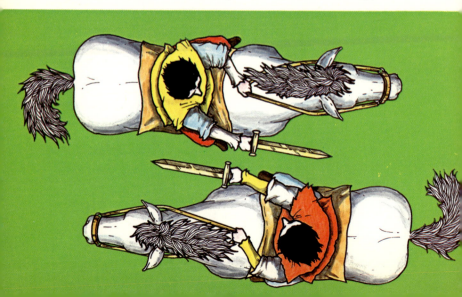

the only countries in Europe to adopt driving on the left when the motor car age dawned. Sweden eventually changed to the right in 1967, in spite of a great deal of opposition.

It would be a complicated procedure for Britain to change to the right, as there are so many vehicles and so many miles of roads involved. All the road signs would have to be moved, and many of them changed altogether. The great majority of the roads would have to be altered as well. Motorways would not be affected to any great extent for the new ones are designed so that they can be used for either system. But the biggest reason for not changing is one of simple economics – it would cost too much. When the Swedes changed in 1967 it cost them thirty million pounds, it would cost Britain a great deal more. And in any case, the British are greatly renowned for their eccentricity so it seems only logical that we should retain that image of being slightly different and remain driving on the left!

## Speed limits

Speed limits are set at sensible levels to ensure the safety of all road users. To exceed the limits is against the law.

On a motorway the maximum allowable speed is 70 miles per hour (112 kilometres per hour); on most dual carriageways the limit is also 70 miles per hour, and this reduces to 60 miles per hour (96 kilometres per hour) on A roads, and to 50 miles per hour (80 kilometres per hour) on other roads. In built-up areas the speed limit is indicated to the driver by signs: here the limit is usually 30 miles per hour (48 kilometres per hour) but in some places of particular danger this may be reduced even further.

Exceeding the speed limit is dangerous and irresponsible. The police try to combat speeding by setting up 'speed traps' to keep a watchful eye open for offending drivers. In the past such traps consisted of two policemen, positioned some distance apart, with stop-watches. It was their job to time motorists over a measured distance to see if they were exceeding the limit. This method, even at its best, proved unreliable due to the time taken for the policemen to react to the situation. Even a person with very quick reflexes is unlikely to achieve an accurate result using this method.

Nowadays the police will either trail a suspected vehicle by motorcycle or car to assess the motorist's speed by checking their own, or they will use a radar device. With the trail method the police will follow the motorist at an even distance for about three tenths of a mile to check the speed.

If you pass a police car parked at the side of the road with its boot open it could be an indication that a radar device is being used to check the speed of the traffic. Concealed in the boot is an instrument called PETA. The initials stand for Portable Electronic Traffic Analyser. It sends out a radio beam across the road and, when a car passes through the beam, a signal is reflected back to the instrument which converts the

Two ways in which VASCAR works.

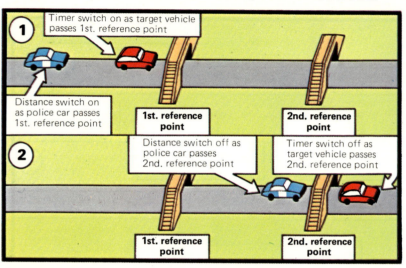

1. Timer switch on as target vehicle passes 1st. reference point

Distance switch on as police car passes 1st. reference point

**1st. reference point**

**2nd. reference point**

2. Distance switch off as police car passes 2nd. reference point

Timer switch off as target vehicle passes 2nd. reference point

**1st. reference point**

**2nd. reference point**

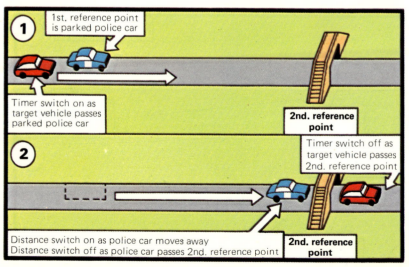

1. 1st. reference point is parked police car

Timer switch on as target vehicle passes parked police car

**2nd. reference point**

2. Timer switch off as target vehicle passes 2nd. reference point

Distance switch on as police car moves away
Distance switch off as police car passes 2nd. reference point

**2nd. reference point**

signal into a miles per hour reading on a meter monitored by a policeman.

There is a new method being introduced into police forces throughout the country for the detection of speeding offences. It is called VASCAR and its name stands for Visual Average Speed Computer and Recorder. There are three parts to the device: a control panel affixed to the dashboard of the police car; an odometer module connected between the speedometer cable and the speedometer to record the distance used for the check; and the computer.

The control panel has a visual display which shows the average speed of the vehicle being checked. Also on the panel are a number of switches that control the operation of VASCAR. Built in to the system is a 'fail-safe' device which prevents the speed on one vehicle being added to another, and which also operates if the equipment should go wrong for any reason.

To operate VASCAR the police driver first measures the distance from a predetermined reference point (often a bridge, but any stationary object may be used), to a second reference point, which can be another stationary object or the police car itself. When the vehicle to be checked reaches the first reference point the operator turns on a time switch, and switches it off when the second reference point is reached. The average speed of the vehicle

being checked (the target vehicle) is then automatically computed and displayed on the visual panel.

This is only one way that the device can be used, for it does not make any difference in which order the various readings are taken. This **is a fact that makes VASCAR much more versatile than any other method for checking speed.** Provided that the police car travels (and records automatically on the computer) the same distance as the target vehicle the actual measurement of the distance can be done at any speed and at any time.

There are five basic methods of operation but each method is capable of several variations:

1 Police car follows target vehicle.
2 Police car is ahead of target vehicle.
3 Police car travelling in the opposite direction to the target vehicle.
4 Police car stationary.
5 Measurement made over a predetermined distance.

At first sight it would seem that this system is open to the same objections as the stop-watch method, namely that the reaction speed of the operator will cause the method to be inaccurate. It has been proved, in tests, however, that even if there is a slight error in operating the switches it does not greatly affect the final result. To further reduce any errors the officers using the equipment have to receive special intensive training.

# Road markings

## White lines

White lines on the road warn the driver of possible dangers, or give a specific order that has to be obeyed.

**Single white line along the road**
Where the traffic is to be divided into several lanes, the lanes are marked by short white lines with long gaps in between the markings. A longer broken white line is placed along the centre of most roads to help the driver keep to the correct side of the road. When the road nears a bend or other hazard the central white lines become much longer with small gaps in between. As the road bends the line becomes continuous, and the driver is not allowed to cross this line. Similar continuous lines are to be seen at the edge of the road on bends and at hazards.

Another white marking that you will often see painted on roadways takes the form of a large arrow. This is a direction sign telling the driver to move into another lane, or to indicate the correct traffic flow.

**Double white line along the road**
A double white line along the centre of the road must not be crossed under any circumstances, both because it is dangerous to do so and because it is against the law. If, however, the line on the driver's side of the road is broken then it is permissible to cross over the continuous line, provided of course that traffic conditions decree that it is safe to do so.

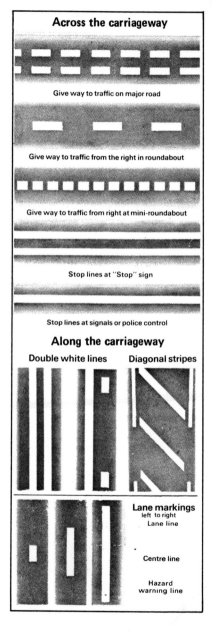

Across the carriageway

Give way to traffic on major road

Give way to traffic from the right in roundabout

Give way to traffic from right at mini-roundabout

Stop lines at "Stop" sign

Stop lines at signals or police control

Along the carriageway

Double white lines          Diagonal stripes

Lane markings
left to right
Lane line

Centre line

Hazard
warning line

A double broken white line with diagonal stripes across the area between the lines, is an area designed to separate various streams of traffic, or to protect vehicles that are turning right. These areas should not be driven over unless it is absolutely essential.

**White lines across the road**
There are also white lines running *across* the road at the approach of a road junction or a roundabout. A double white line indicates that the driver should stop at the junction and ensure that the major road is safe to cross, or join, before proceeding. A single white line is used to halt the traffic at road signals or check points. Double broken lines at a junction indicate to the driver that he must give right of way to the traffic on the major road, and a single broken line is used at the entrance to a roundabout to inform the driver that he must give way to traffic already on the roundabout.

As you approach a roundabout you will often see a series of lines across the road which become closer together the nearer you are to the roundabout. These are designed to remind the driver that he is travelling too fast, so that he reduces his speed to a safe level before entering the roundabout.

**Yellow lines and box junctions**
Yellow lines along the edge of the road provide a general indication of parking restrictions. The exact nature of these restrictions can vary so a notice is used to give the exact times that parking is prohibited.

A broken yellow line means that parking is limited to the times given on the qualifying notice. The plate may state that waiting is limited to a certain period, such as twenty minutes in any one hour, or that waiting is prohibited during certain times of the day.

A continuous single yellow line means that parking is not allowed

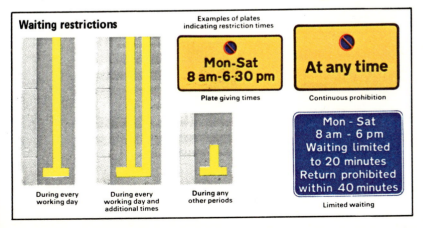

**Waiting restrictions**

Examples of plates indicating restriction times

Mon-Sat 8 am-6·30 pm

Plate giving times

At any time

Continuous prohibition

Mon - Sat 8 am - 6 pm Waiting limited to 20 minutes Return prohibited within 40 minutes

Limited waiting

During every working day

During every working day and additional times

During any other periods

during the working day. Generally this means that parking is prohibited between the hours of 7 am and 7 pm from Monday to Friday. In most cases, however, there is a qualifying notice which gives the exact times during which parking is not permitted, for example: Mon–Sat 8 am–6.30 pm.

Double yellow lines indicate that parking is not allowed during the working day (7 am–7 pm) nor at certain other times as indicated on the qualifying plate. One plate you will see quite often with double yellow lines reads 'At any time'. This simply means that parking is not allowed at all.

Yellow stripes on the *kerb* give a general indication that loading and unloading vehicles is not permitted. A notice nearby will state the exact times that the prohibition is in force.

One stripe means that loading and unloading is prohibited at certain times. These are usually peak periods – times when there is a lot of traffic – such as early morning and late afternoon. A qualifying plate gives the exact times.

Two yellow stripes prohibit loading and unloading during the working day. Again, a plate will qualify the exact times that the prohibition is operative.

Three stripes mean that loading and unloading is not allowed during the working day nor at certain additional times as indicated on the qualifying plate.

When travelling through a town look out for box junctions. These consist of yellow diagonal lines criss-crossing the central area of a

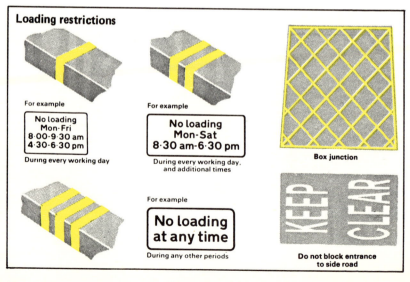

**Loading restrictions**

For example

No loading
Mon-Fri
8.00-9.30 am
4.30-6.30 pm

During every working day

For example

No loading
Mon-Sat
8.30 am-6.30 pm

During every working day, and additional times

**Box junction**

For example

No loading
at any time

During any other periods

KEEP CLEAR

Do not block entrance to side road

crossroads. A driver is not allowed to move on to this area of the road unless he is absolutely sure that his exit is clear. The idea of this box is to improve the flow of traffic and prevent traffic from building up.

## Cat's-eyes

An interesting story surrounds the invention of cat's-eyes. One night Percy Shaw was driving home in the fog. He was having great difficulty in seeing where he was going until he drove through a town in which there were tram lines on the road. There, to his surprise, he found that he could drive quite safely, for his headlights were reflected by the metal lines. His inventive mind immediately reasoned that here was the basis for an idea that could help

to improve safety for drivers on other roads in bad conditions.

After much thought he came up with the idea of having glass studs set into the road. He also developed a self-wiping device so that the studs would be automatically wiped clean every time a vehicle ran over them.

The first reflecting road studs, which most people call cat's-eyes, were installed on the roads in 1934. It was an idea that proved very popular and there are now in excess of seven million studs of various types embedded in the roads of Britain. White studs are used to mark the centre of the road. They are also used to mark out traffic lanes. Along the edges of dual carriageways and motorways you will see red studs, and amber studs are used to mark the central reservation.

## Traffic signs

There are three main shapes of traffic sign: circular, triangular and rectangular.

**Circular signs** give instructions that must be obeyed. They are usually white with a red border, or blue with a white or red border. The red-bordered signs are usually prohibitive signs, in other words they forbid the road user to do certain things. The blue signs with white borders are generally compulsory in that the road user must obey them at all times, even when there appears to be no obvious danger.

The structure of a cat's-eye.

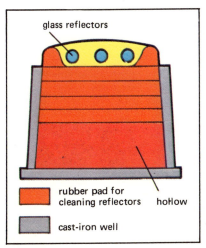

glass reflectors

rubber pad for cleaning reflectors

hollow

cast-iron well

Triangular signs usually have a white background and a red border. They are mainly warning signs, giving the road user an indication of hazards to watch out for. Two notable exceptions are the 'upside-down' triangular 'Stop' and 'Give Way' signs to be seen at the approach to major roads. These are compulsory signs.

Rectangular signs provide either directions or information. Information signs are either white or blue with symbols or lettering in black, white or red. The colours of direction signs vary as follows: those at the approaches to junctions on primary routes have a green background whereas those on other routes have a white background. Some direction signs have a blue border, and these usually give directions to local places. On occasion you will see direction signs on which a road number is given in brackets. This indicates roads that turn off the route indicated.

Regulations laid down by the Secretary of State for the Environment set out the exact size, shape and colour of road signs and only borough, county, and urban district councils are allowed to erect such signs. Thus, people who put 'No

**Road signs**

| Sign | Meaning |
|---|---|
| 40 | Maximum speed |
| | National speed limit applies |
| GIVE WAY | Give way to traffic on major road |
| | Turn left (right if symbol reversed) |
| | Keep left (right if symbol reversed) |
| STOP CHILDREN | School crossing patrol |
| | No entry for vehicular traffic |
| | No right turn |
| | No left turn |
| | No U turns |
| | Ahead only |
| | Turn left ahead (right if symbol reversed) |
| | No overtaking |
| | No vehicles |
| | No motor vehicles |
| | No motor vehicles except solo motorcycles scooters or mopeds |
| | No vehicles with over 12 seats except regular scheduled, school and works buses |
| | Vehicles may pass either side to reach same destination |
| | Route to be used by pedal cyclists only |
| | No cycling |
| 3 tons | No goods vehicles over unladen weight shown (unladen weight limit) |
| 10 TONS | No vehicles, including load, over weight shown (total weight limit) |
| 14'6" | No vehicles over height shown |
| 32 feet | No vehicle or combination of vehicles over length shown |
| 30 | Minimum speed |
| 30 | End of minimum speed |
| 7'6" | No vehicles over width shown |
| | No stopping (Clearway) |
| | Give priority to vehicles from opposite direction |
| URBAN CLEARWAY Monday to Friday am 8·9 30 pm 4 30 6 30 | No stopping during times shown except for up to 2 mins. to set down or pick up passengers |
| | Mini-roundabout (roundabout circulation – give way to vehicles from the immediate right) |
| | One-way traffic (Compare circular "Ahead only" sign |

Parking' or 'No Turning' notices outside their property are, strictly speaking, breaking the law. In fact they could be prosecuted for erecting such signs but this rarely happens in actual practice.

Notable exceptions to the law regarding the placing of signs are the temporary direction signs erected by the Automobile Association and the Royal Automobile Club. Such signs, blue and white for the RAC, and yellow and black for the AA, bear the association's insignia as well as the direction, and are usually put up for special events such as a gymkhana, race meeting, or a circus.

Other signs give directions to places of interest such as stately homes.

During the holiday season particular routes are signposted to enable road users to avoid areas of possible traffic congestion. Diversion signs are erected when there is an accident, if the road is under repair, or presents some other hazard. The motoring organisations have special permission to erect such signs as one of the many services that they provide for their members. In fact in the early days of motoring the only signs to provide information for the road user were those of the motoring organisations.

## Old signposts

Modern direction signs conform to the design of those found on the Continent. They have been designed so that they can be easily read by a motorist travelling by at speed. It is still, however, possible to find older signposts, particularly in country areas, which comprise several arms pointing the direction to be taken. Some are made of metal but it is also possible to find many made from wood.

To find really old direction signs it is best to look at the side of the road. If you keep your eyes open you will be surprised to find quite a number of old mileposts, giving the distance to several places. If the stone is very old you will observe that the distance appears to be less than modern distances. Apart from the fact that measuring distances is more accurate today than it was in the past, these differences often arise because the olden-day mile consisted of 10 furlongs (a furlong is 201 metres or 220 yards) whereas the modern mile is made up of only 8 furlongs.

## Traffic lights

Traffic lights are an indispensable safety aid on modern roads and it is essential that every road user is familiar with their sequence, which is shown on this page.

The first traffic lights in Britain were installed outside the Houses of

The sequence in which traffic lights operate. Red means 'stop'. Red and amber together also means 'stop'. Green means go if the way is clear. Amber showing by itself warns vehicles to stop unless to do so would cause an accident. A green arrow means that you may go in the direction shown by the arrow.

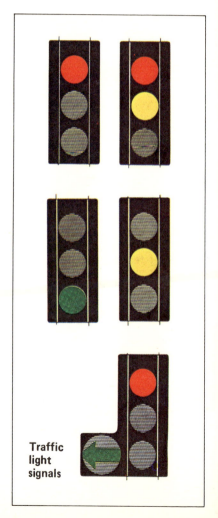

**Traffic light signals**

Parliament, London, in 1868. They were designed by John Knight, a railway signalling engineer, and looked very much like the semaphore signals used by the railways. They were not very popular, and were short-lived because one day they blew up. A policeman was killed in the explosion and it was to be almost fifty years before traffic lights were again seen in London.

The new traffic lights were situated at the junction of St James's Street and Piccadilly, and were controlled by a policeman in a signal box in the centre of the road. These signals proved to be very successful and other signal traffic lights were installed at other busy junctions. It was not long before lights had been designed that were automatic, being controlled by a timing mechanism. The first of this type were installed in Wolverhampton for what was intended to be a one-day trial period, but they were so successful that they remained there for forty years.

Modern lights can even adjust the timing of the signals in accordance with the density of the road traffic.

## Railway level crossings

There are three main types of railway level crossings that you may encounter during your travels around the British Isles: open crossings; crossings with gates or full barriers; and automatic crossings with half barriers.

Open crossings are those in which

Three types of level crossing. *Top:* Gated *Centre:* Full barrier. *Bottom:* Automatic half barrier.

the railway line simply crosses the road. Some of these have flashing red stop lights to warn the traffic that a train is due, but there are others which do not have any warning system. The same applies to crossings with gates that go right across the road. Some have no warning system and it is up to the road user to ensure that the way is clear before opening the gates, crossing, and then closing the gates. The majority of gate crossings do, however, have small red and green, or flashing red, warning lights to signify the approach of a train, and in many cases the gates are opened and closed by an attendant.

Modern crossings are automatic. They have a barrier that goes halfway across the road and this is opened and closed automatically by the trains as they approach and go away from the crossing. Flashing red stop lights and bells are used to warn the road user that the barrier is about to come down.

## Bridges

Although bridges are of many different designs they can be divided into three basic types: beam, arch and suspension. The type of bridge selected for any particular site will depend upon the distance to be

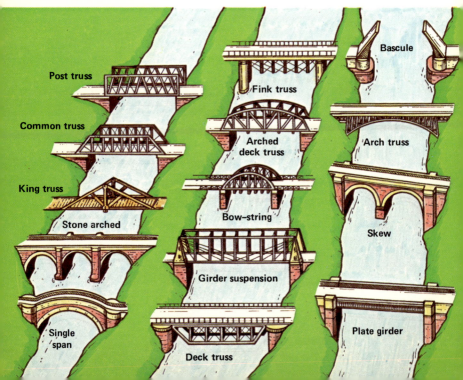

Post truss

Common truss

King truss

Stone arched

Single span

Fink truss

Arched deck truss

Bow–string

Girder suspension

Deck truss

Bascule

Arch truss

Skew

Plate girder

...ed, the type of traffic that will
...using it, the depth of the valley or
...ver to be traversed, and whether
the ground is hard or soft.

**Beam bridges**, sometimes known
as girder bridges, are the simplest
type of bridge and consist of a beam
of timber or steel supported at each
end by piers. As the beam will
collapse if too much weight is placed
upon it, long bridges of this type
must be supported by building
additional piers. In cases where the
beam is made of wood or metal, it is
sometimes formed into interlocked
trellises. This variation is known as a
*truss bridge*.

Cantilever bridges are a variation
of the beam bridge and usually
consist of two beams fixed to either
bank of the area to be traversed, and
supported by piers. There is often a
third beam connecting the two piers.
This central beam is called the
*suspended span*. The most famous steel
cantilever bridge in the British Isles
is the Forth Railway Bridge in
Scotland. It was designed by Sir
Benjamin Baker in 1890. Some
modern cantilever bridges are made
with reinforced concrete.

**Arch bridges** are usually made of
brick or stone and, as their name
implies, are formed of arches. The
arches can support a greater weight
than the normal simple beam bridge

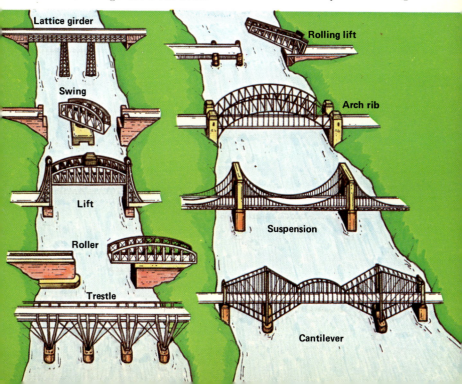

Lattice girder
Rolling lift
Swing
Arch rib
Lift
Roller
Suspension
Trestle
Cantilever

because the angled arches have great strength. Arch bridges can also be constructed of iron and steel, the first iron bridge of this type (in fact the first iron bridge of any type) being built at Coalbrookdale in 1779. It is now one of the features of the Ironbridge Gorge Open Air Museum. The famous bridge over the River Tyne at Newcastle is also a steel arch bridge.

**Suspension bridges** have a beam which is supported by steel cables suspended from high towers. Many modern road bridges are of this type. The cables are made of thousands of steel wires and can be anything up to a metre (3·28 feet) thick.

Among modern suspension bridges are the Forth Road Bridge, which has a span of 1006 metres (3,300 feet) and was opened in 1964, and the Severn road bridge, near Bristol, which has a span of 988 metres (3,240 feet) and was designed

by Sir Gilbert Roberts, was ope[...] in 1966.

The Forth Road Bridge contain[...] 39,000 tonnes of steel and 114,675 cubic metres (150,000 cubic yards) of concrete. An unusual feature of the bridge when it was built was three holes spaced at intervals along the bridge. These allow the wind to rush through it instead of forcing it up. If the holes were not there the bridge could be in danger of breaking in bad weather. Even so, the bridge will move some 7 metres (23 feet) in a high wind, although this is allowed for in the design. Another factor that had to be taken into consideration by the bridge designers was temperature. On a cold day the centre of the bridge can be up to $1\frac{1}{2}$ metres (5 feet) higher in the centre than it is on a warm day!

At present the longest suspension bridge is the Verrazano Narrows Bridge across the entrance to New

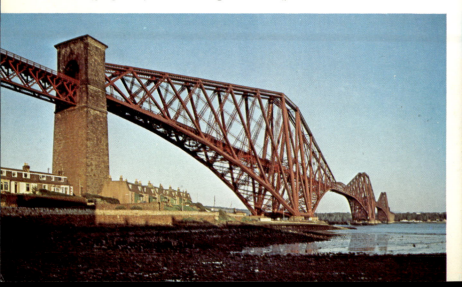

York Harbour in America (1,298 metres or 4,257 feet) but when the Humber Bridge is opened in 1979 Great Britain will hold the record with a span of 1,410 metres (4,625 feet). In addition to the main span there will be two side spans, that on the north bank being 280 metres (918 feet) long, and that to the south having a length of 530 metres (1,738 feet). A short viaduct will link the north side of the bridge with the administration and toll area and beyond that there will be an interchange with the A63. There will also be an approach viaduct to the south side of the bridge. This will come from an interchange with the A1077.

## Other bridges

Some bridges are constructed so that they can move to allow shipping to pass by. These include swing bridges, where the central beam moves on a pivot, lift bridges in which the whole of the central beam is lifted up, and bascule bridges in which only one end of the beam is lifted, the other end remaining connected to the ground.

Examples of swing bridges can be seen at Newcastle-upon-Tyne, and Kincardine in Scotland. A lift bridge can be seen on the Tees at Middlesbrough. The best known bascule bridge in Britain is Tower Bridge in London which has two 1,000 tonne bascules. It was first opened in 1894 and until 1973 used the original hydraulic machinery to lift the bascules.

Not all the bridges mentioned are used for road traffic, but you should at least be able to see bridges of each type during your travels.

*Opposite:* Forth rail bridge, Scotland. *Below left:* Clifton suspension bridge, Bristol. *Below right:* Swing bridge (foreground) and steel arch bridge at Newcastle upon Tyne.

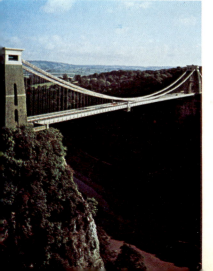

## Tunnels under rivers

| Name | River | Location |
|------|-------|----------|
| Blackwall | Thames | 4·8 kilometres (3 miles) east of Tower Bridge |
| Clyde | Clyde | Whiteinch near Glasgow |
| Dartford | Thames | 24 kilometres (15 miles) east of Tower Bridge |
| Mersey | Mersey | Liverpool and Birkenhead |
| Rotherhithe | Thames | 1·6 kilometres (1 mile) east of Tower Bridge |
| Tyne | Tyne | Newcastle |

## Tolls

Modern examples of the old toll roads can be found at the entry of new bridges and road tunnels, at which road users are charged a fee for use. It is still possible, however, to find examples of ancient toll roads where fees still have to be paid. Many of these tolls exist because the road passes across private land, but there are also a few which come under the jurisdiction of local authorities. The history of some of the existing tolls is well documented.

At Swinford in Oxfordshire King George III got his feet wet whilst crossing the River Thames by ferry. He gave the Earl of Abingdon permission to collect a tax-free toll if he built a bridge over the river at that point, and the Earl's family still collect a toll from everyone who crosses.

A similar toll is that at Old Wooden Bridge, Selby, Yorkshire.

This toll dates from the eighteenth century. The government of the day said that any person who erected a bridge across the River Ouse at that point would be entitled to charge a toll for its use and that all the fees received would be free of income tax. They still are.

Another toll can be found at Warburton Bridge, Lymm, Cheshire. In the nineteenth century this was a bridge over the River Mersey. The river was diverted and the bed built up so that it now forms an ordinary road – but it is still necessary to pay the hundred-year-old toll if you want to travel on this road.

There are several other toll bridges and roads dotted around the country. Drivers tend to resent having to pay the toll, but using an alternative route will often result in a longer journey and a great loss of time.

The toll bridge at Whitchurch, Oxfordshire.

## Toll bridges

| Name of bridge | Location |
| --- | --- |
| Clifton | Avon |
| Connel | Strathclyde |
| Dunham | Lincolnshire |
| Forth | Lothian |
| Lymington | Hampshire |
| Middlesbrough | Yorkshire |
| Newport | Gwent |
| Old Shoreham | Sussex |
| Penrhyndeu-draeth | Gwynedd |
| Portmadoc | Gwynedd |
| Sandwich | Kent |
| Selby | Yorkshire |
| Severn | Avon/Gwent |
| Swinford | Oxfordshire |
| Shard | Lancashire |
| Tamar | Devon |
| Tay | Fife/Tayside |
| Warburton | Cheshire |
| **Whitchurch** | Oxfordshire |
| Whitney | Hereford and Worcester |

## Ferries

In spite of the advance in bridge and tunnel construction in recent years there are still many places where ferries operate to take vehicles across expanses of water. To cross a river or lake by ferry can be an interesting and unusual experience, so it is worth keeping a look out for them. The locations of some of the principal ferries in the British Isles are listed opposite. Many of these ferries are only in operation during parts of the year so it is as well to check before the start of your journey or you may have a long trip to the nearest bridge.

## Ferries to the Continent

Dover—Boulogne
Dover—Boulogne (Hovercraft)
Dover—Calais
Dover—Dunkirk
Dover—Ostend
Dover—Zeebrugge
Felixstowe—Antwerp
Felixstowe—Rotterdam (Europort)
Harwich—Bremerhaven
Harwich—Esbjerg
Harwich—Hamburg
Harwich—Hook of Holland
Harwich—Kristiansand
Harwich—Ostend
Hull—Gothenburg
Hull—Rotterdam (Europort)
Immingham—Amsterdam
Immingham—Gothenburg
Newcastle—Bergen
Newcastle—Stavanger
Newhaven—Dieppe
Ramsgate—Calais (Hovercraft)
Rosslare—Le Havre
Southampton—Cherbourg
Southampton—Le Havre
Tilbury—Gothenburg

*Inset:* A cross-channel car ferry.

## Ferries to the islands

Ardrossan (Strathclyde)—Brodick (Arran)
Ardrossan (Strathclyde)—Douglas (Isle of Man)
Kennacraig (Strathclyde)—Port Askaig (Islay)
Liverpool (Merseyside)—Douglas (Isle of Man)
Lymington (Hampshire)—Yarmouth (Isle of Wight)
Mallaig (Highland)—Armadale (Skye)
Mallaig (Highland)—Lochboisdale (South Uist)—Castlebay (Barra)
Oban (Strathclyde)—Craignure (Mull)—Lochaline (Highland)
Southampton (Hampshire)—Cowes (Isle of Wight)
Uig (Strathclyde)—Lochmaddy (North Uist)
Uig (Skye)—Tarbert (Lewis)
Ullapool (Highland)—Stornaway (Lewis)
West Loch Tarbert (Harris)—Gigha—Port Ellen (Islay)
West Loch Tarbert (Harris)—Jura—Port Askaig (Islay)—Colonsay

## Ferries to Ireland

Ardrossan (Strathclyde)—Belfast
Campbeltown (Strathclyde)—Red Bay
Fishguard (Dyfed)—Rosslare (Wexford)
Heysham (Lancashire)—Belfast
Heysham (Lancashire)—Dun Laoghaire (Dublin)
Holyhead (Gwynedd)—Dun Laoghaire (Dublin)
Liverpool (Merseyside)—Belfast
Liverpool (Merseyside)—Dublin
Preston (Lancashire)—Larne (Antrim)
Stranraer (Dumfries) and Galloway—Larne (Antrim)
Swansea (Glamorgan)—Cork

## Inland Ferries

Ballachulish (Highland)
Corran—Ardgour (Highland)
Dartmouth—Kingswear (Devon)
Dartmouth—Old Rock (Devon)
Dittisham—Greenway (Devon)
Dunoon—Gourock (Strathclyde)
Erskine—Old Kilpatrick
   (Glasgow, Strathclyde)
Fowey—Bodinnick (Cornwall)
Hull—New Holland (Humberside)
Kessock (Highland)
King Harry—Philleigh (Cornwall)
Kylesku (Highland)
Neyland—Hobbs Point (Dyfed)
Reedham (Norfolk)
Renfrew—Yoker
   (Glasgow, Strathclyde)
Sandbanks—Shell Bay (Dorset)
South Shields—North Shields
   (Tyne and Wear)
Strome (Highland)
Torpoint—Devonport (Cornwall)
Windermere (Cumbria)
Woolston—Southampton
   (Hampshire)
Woolwich—North Woolwich
   (London)

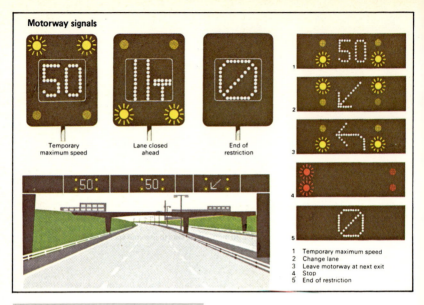

Motorway signals

Temporary maximum speed

Lane closed ahead

End of restriction

1 Temporary maximum speed
2 Change lane
3 Leave motorway at next exit
4 Stop
5 End of restriction

# On the motorway

Motorways are roads with two or more lanes of traffic in each direction. They are prohibited to certain types of vehicle. At the start of all motorways you will see a sign setting out the types of vehicles, such as bicycles, motorcycles under 50 cc capacity, agricultural vehicles, certain invalid carriages and horse-drawn vehicles, that are not permitted on the motorway. Other rules applicable to motorways are that you must not stop or reverse on the carriageway. Neither must you stop on the central reserve or on the hard shoulder. Parking on the hard shoulder is permitted only in the case of an emergency. As with other roads it is against the law to exceed the speed limit prescribed for the motorway or any special limit laid down for the specific vehicle.

As traffic travels faster on a motorway than on other roads the traffic signs have been specially designed so that they can be easily read whilst travelling at speed. They are much larger than ordinary direction signs and consist of white lettering on a blue background. Information signs on the motorway are of the same colouring and design.

## Warning signals

Many motorways have flashing amber light signals to warn of dangerous conditions ahead. When the lights are flashing it means that drivers should keep their speed down below 30 mph (48 kph) until they have passed the danger area.

*Above left:* Warning signals to be seen on motorways. *Above right:* Gravelly Hill interchange, better known as Spaghetti Junction, on the M6 near Birmingham.

Remote-controlled signals will eventually be placed on the central reserve of all rural motorways. These will consist of a square sign with an amber light at each of the four corners, and a panel in the centre. When the lights are flashing the central panel contains information or instructions for the road user. Such signals will be placed at two-mile (3·2 kilometre) intervals along the motorway.

On urban motorways the signals are placed above the road so that each lane has its own individual signal. These signals, which will eventually be positioned at least every 900 metres (2,950 feet), have four flashing lights and a central illuminated panel. The two outermost lights of each set of four are red, the inner two are amber. The amber lights are used to warn the driver, and the red lights are an order to stop.

## Interchanges

An interchange is the point at which traffic may leave or join the motorway. As you approach an interchange on a motorway there are usually three direction signs, placed at intervals of one mile (1·6 kilometres), half a mile (0·8 kilometres), and a quarter of a mile (0·4 kilometres) from the exit road. The first of these signs is the smallest, and they gradually increase in size, each sign giving a little more information than the previous sign.

Each interchange is also marked with its own number; this means that a traveller can tell by looking at his map exactly which interchange he is approaching. In this way he can plan and follow his route.

As you approach or leave a motorway look out for two interesting features. Firstly, as you approach the interchange, or the end of the motorway, you will see three signs at the side of the road. They consist of three, two and then one diagonal stripes on a blue background. The number of stripes tells the driver the distance in 100 yard (30·5 metre) intervals to the exit road. Secondly, roads on to the motorway always slope downwards and exit roads always slope upwards. This is to help drivers adjust their driving speed to the change of conditions. The downhill road on the motorway enables the motorist to quickly reach the speed of the traffic on the motorway, and the uphill road helps the motorist slow down quickly when leaving the motorway.

Although it is not always possible from a car to see the various patterns formed by the complete interchange you will, if you keep your eyes open, be able to discern the form that the interchange takes. Each of these forms has a special name as shown in the diagrams on the right of this page.

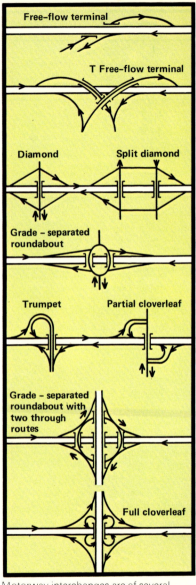

Motorway interchanges are of several basic types, some of which are shown.

## Emergency telephones

When you are travelling along a motorway look out for the emergency telephones which are set at one-mile (1·6 kilometre) intervals along the side of the road. You will notice that they are set in pairs, one on each side of the motorway. On the side of the telephone casing is a letter and a number, the number indicates the distance in miles from the start of the motorway. This number is relayed to the police when using the emergency telephone so they can instantly locate the position of the emergency. Two types of roadside telephone can be seen; the older variety are in large blue boxes with a white sign on the outside and the newer type consist of smaller yellow boxes that hold the telephone handset. The old type have only one-way communication – you can telephone the police but they cannot ring you back, whereas the newer type can be used in either direction. Instructions for the use of the telephones are given in the box and are written in English, French, and German.

## Motorway markers

You should also keep a look out for motorway markers alongside the motorway. These posts are white, with a red reflector strip near the top. On the side of these are two numbers. The top number indicates the number of miles from the zero reference point. This point is often the start of the motorway but there are exceptions. With unfinished motorways the zero reference point may be the start of the motorway when the work is completed, and with motorways starting from London the zero reference point is Charing Cross. The lower of the two numbers shows the number of hectometres (100 metres or 328 feet) from the last telephone. On the side of the post is a small picture of a telephone and an arrow pointing to the nearest emergency telephone. Other markers will be seen on the central reserve, and these are blue with a white reflector strip.

The old (left) and the new emergency telephones on the motorway.

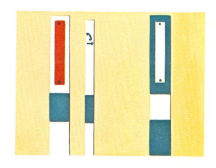

Boundary markers can be seen at the edge of the motorway and on the central reserve.

## Garages and service stations

### Repairs and servicing

At some garages you will see AA symbols on which there are either one, two or three spanners. The number of spanners indicates the level of motor car repairs that the garage is qualified to handle. Three spanners means that the garage is capable of tackling almost every mechanical, electrical, or body repair, or vehicle overhaul. Two spanners are given to those garages that are competent to handle standard repairs and servicing but which are less well equipped than those with three spanners. One spanner indicates that the garage can carry out routine servicing and repairs of a minor nature.

You may also see an AA sign bearing a breakdown truck or a motorcycle. The breakdown truck is shown at garages that participate in a free breakdown service provided by the AA for its members. The motorcycle emblem is shown at garages that specialise in the repair and servicing of motorcycles, scooters and three-wheeled vehicles.

### M.o.T. test

A blue sign on which there are three white triangles signifies that the garage is authorised to carry out the Department of the Environment annual vehicle test. This is still often referred to as the M.o.T. (Ministry of Transport) test. This test must be carried out annually on all cars registered in the British Isles that are over three years old. With cars that have been used abroad and then registered in this country the test may be required at an earlier date.

The purpose of the test is to establish that the vehicle is roadworthy and that the legal requirements for brakes, lights, steering, seat belts, tyres, and so on have been met.

### Petrol grades

On the petrol pumps at a garage you will see a number of stars displayed. These indicate the grade of petrol supplied by each pump. Some pumps, known as 'blender pumps', supply all grades. To obtain a specific grade a selector handle must be moved to the particular grade required.

The grade of petrol is expressed in octane rating. This is a rating based on the amount of compression that the fuel will withstand before the mixture explodes prematurely, i.e. before the spark plug fires. This pre-ignition is called 'knocking' and the octane rating is often referred to as the amount of 'anti-knock' property in the fuel.

The rating required for modern cars must be at least 80 octane, but the most suitable grade for a particular vehicle is determined to a great extent by the compression ratio of the engine. The higher the compression ratio the higher the grade of petrol required. Motor car manufacturers state the most suitable grade to be used for each model they produce, and motorists are advised to use the recommended grade.

The octane rating for each of the star grades are as follows:

    **\*\*** minimum rating of 90 octane

   **\*\*\*** minimum rating of 94 octane

  **\*\*\*\*** rating of between 97 and 99 octane

**\*\*\*\*\*** minimum rating of 100 octane

**Brands** When the motorist requires petrol he is faced with a large number of different brands. Next time you are on the road see how many different brands of petrol you can see. You will also find that most petrol producers have a symbol to make their garages easily recognisable. Some of the symbols you may see are shown on the following page. In addition to the company symbols, garages that are owned by a particular company are usually painted in distinctive colours. The colours are normally standard for each garage within the group. Here are the colours that some groups use. See how many more you can discover.

| | |
|---|---|
| *BP* | green and yellow |
| *Esso* | red, white and blue |
| *Heron* | red and yellow |
| *Jet* | yellow and black |
| *National* | blue and yellow |
| *Shell* | red and yellow |

*Left:* Look out for these symbols when you pass a garage.

51

**Type of pump** As you pass each garage take a look at the petrol pumps. You will find there are quite a variety of types. In country areas you may well see pumps that are very old. It is even possible to find garages where the petrol has to be pumped from the storage tank by hand. In modern garages the petrol is drawn into the pump by electricity.

More and more garages are changing to automatic pumps where the driver serves himself. Again, you will find that there are several different types. With some, the driver must put a pound note into a special part of the pump itself before he can obtain any petrol. With

*Above:* Symbols used by some of the well-known petrol companies.

*Below:* Petrol pumps come in many shapes and sizes. The latest type, shown on the right, provides a digital display of the quantity of fuel bought and the total price.

others, the amount of petrol taken is recorded in the office at the garage and the driver has to go into the office to pay the required amount.

## It's a mirage!

When out travelling on a hot day you may see what appear to be pools of water on the road ahead. Occasionally it is possible to see trees or other objects apparently floating upside down in the water! But when you get closer the scene disappears. What you are actually seeing in each case is a mirage – formed in the same way as mirages are formed in hot desert regions.

What happens is that the sun heats up the surface of the road, which in turn warms the air in contact with it. As a result the air near the road is of a different density to the layer of air immediately above it. On a really warm day there may

in fact be several air layers, each layer being of a higher density to the one below it. Some of the light rays travelling through these various layers are reflected, in the same way that some of the light travelling through water or a lens is reflected. When this happens a mirror effect is produced, and this is what we see as a shimmering pool of water on the road.

## Rules for pedestrians

The two principal rules for pedestrians are see and be seen, and learn respect for the road. If walking along a road where there is no footpath the pedestrian should be on the right-hand side of the road, facing the oncoming traffic. Where there is a pavement, use it. To make

How the rays of light are bent to form a mirage.

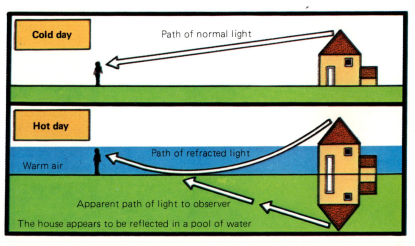

**Cold day** — Path of normal light

**Hot day** — Path of refracted light
Warm air
Apparent path of light to observer
The house appears to be reflected in a pool of water

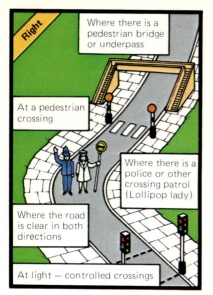

Right

Where there is a pedestrian bridge or underpass

At a pedestrian crossing

Where there is a police or other crossing patrol (Lollipop lady)

Where the road is clear in both directions

At light – controlled crossings

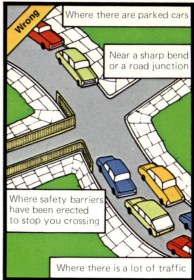

Wrong

Where there are parked cars

Near a sharp bend or a road junction

Where safety barriers have been erected to stop you crossing

Where there is a lot of traffic

sure that you can be seen at night wear light-coloured or reflective clothing. It is also a good idea to carry a light. A group of pedestrians on the road at night should carry a white light at the front of the group and a red light at the rear.

Pedestrians should observe the kerb drill. They should look both ways to ensure the road is clear before crossing. This applies even when crossing a one-way street for it is possible that a driver has made a mistake and is travelling in the wrong direction.

If crossings are provided they should be used – even if it does mean walking a little further than necessary. When using a crossing, however, the rule of see and be seen still applies. A pedestrian should not step straight off the pavement on to the crossing and expect the traffic to stop automatically. The pedestrian should always allow oncoming traffic sufficient time to slow down or stop before crossing the road.

## The green cross code

1 First find a safe place to cross, then stop.

2 Stand on the pavement near the kerb.

3 Look all round for traffic and listen.

4 If traffic is coming, let it pass. Look all round again and listen.

5 When there is no traffic near, walk straight across the road.

6 Keep looking and listening for traffic while you cross.

## Pedestrian crossings

Zebra crossings consist of black-and-white stripes marked across the road. They provide a safe crossing place for pedestrians. Traffic islands are sometimes placed in the centre of wide roads at a zebra crossing. This means that the pedestrian can cross the road in two separate stages, concentrating on just one direction of traffic at a time. You will also note that these crossings are marked by Belisha beacons – tall striped poles with an orange globular flashing light on the top. These beacons are named after Lord Hore-Belisha who introduced them in 1934. The flashing variety was, in 1953, made compulsory to mark zebra crossings.

Some crossings are controlled by push-button signals at the side of the road. At these the pedestrian has to press the button and then wait for a lighted signal – a green pedestrian – that tells him that it is safe to cross. This type of crossing is connected to a system of traffic lights; an amber signal indicates that the driver must stop, but a flashing amber light permits the driver to proceed provided that there are no pedestrians on the crossing.

*Left:* Pedestrians should cross the road in safe places, such as those shown on the left. Those on the right are dangerous.
*Below:* A 'pelican' crossing on a one-way street.

# Hints for cyclists

When buying a bicycle it is important to choose one that is most suited to your needs. It is no use buying a bicycle intended for shopping expeditions if your main intention is to use it for touring and holiday outings. The wisest thing to do is to ask the advice of the salesman in the shop.

Always maintain your bicycle in good condition. It will give you more pleasure that way and it will cost less in the long run. If you do not know how to look after a bicycle properly get a good book on the subject – you'll find one in your local bookshop or library. Check the brakes, tyres and lights regularly. Carry a puncture outfit and some spanners in a saddle bag, in case of breakdowns. It is also worthwhile putting a waterproof cape in the saddle bag as well.

When on the road remember the following:

1 If there is a special cycle track alongside the road use it. If not, use the road but keep to the left-hand side.

2 Keep in single file, especially on busy roads and in country lanes.

3 Never ride on the pavement.

4 Do not hold on to a vehicle or another cyclist, and do not ride too close to another vehicle.

5 Make sure that you can see exactly what you are doing at all times and also ensure that you yourself can be seen. Never approach on the inside of other vehicles.

6 Always signal clearly and in good time.

7 Consider other road users.

8 Read the Highway Code.

Accessories and tools that every cyclist should have available.

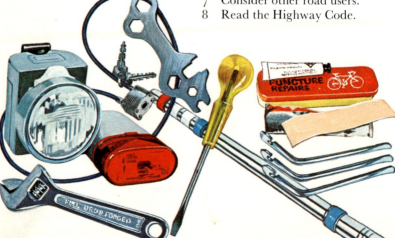

# The Motor Car

## How it works

### Petrol engine

The modern motor car engine is started by turning a key in the ignition switch. This connects the electric current from the battery to the electrical system of the car. The electric current passes to the starter motor and turns a large, heavy wheel called the flywheel. The flywheel is attached to the end of the crankshaft, to which are also attached the pistons. The pistons travel up and down inside the main part of the engine, called the block. As the starter motor turns the crankshaft, one of the pistons travels down its cylinder, sucking in a mixture of petrol and air. (The petrol and air mixture is produced by the carburettor.) The mixture is allowed to enter the cylinder by the opening of a special valve called an inlet valve which is present in each cylinder.

As the inlet valve opens, the piston travelling down the cylinder draws in the petrol and air mixture; this is called the *induction stroke*. Next, the inlet valve closes, sealing the cylinder, and the piston moves back up the cylinder, compressing the mixture as it does so. This is called the *compression stroke*. Now, with the piston almost at the end of its upward travel, electricity is supplied to the sparking plug situated in the top of the cylinder. The electricity sparks across the electrode of the sparking plug, causing an explosion of the mixture in the cylinder. This forces the piston back down the cylinder, and is called the *power stroke*. The power stroke revolves the crankshaft to which all the pistons are connected, and brings each to its own position in the stroke cycle. After the power stroke comes the *exhaust stroke*, and at this point the second valve, the exhaust valve, opens in the top of the cylinder allowing burnt gases to escape from the cylinder, as the piston moves back up to start the cycle again.

The sequence of valve opening and closing for each cylinder is controlled by a shaft called the camshaft. The camshaft revolves and pushes long rods called tappets, up and down to activate the valves within the cylinder head. Thus each piston goes through a continuous 4-cycled sequence of strokes. Such engines are called 4-stroke engines. This process, also called the Otto cycle after its inventor, is repeated continuously by each piston in turn, and the repetitive action by all the pistons in sequence keeps the crankshaft turning.

As only one of the four strokes actually turns the crankshaft, it is necessary to have some means of keeping the crankshaft revolving until the next power stroke. This is accomplished by means of the flywheel which, in effect, stores the energy produced by the explosion at the top of the cylinder to help keep the crankshaft turning and the pistons continuing their strokes. The storage of energy is rather like that of a top that continues to spin even though the force that started it has finished.

The crankshaft's turning action, via the gearbox, provides the motive power to turn the driving wheels. With rear-wheel drive cars the wheels are turned through a long rod called the propshaft connected to the gearbox; and in front-wheel drive cars by the drive shafts. At the front end of the crankshaft is a pulley which turns, by means of a belt, a fan to cool the radiator containing water. This water is then pumped round the cylinder block to cool the engine. Some cars have an electric fan so do not need a fan belt or pulley. Others have a fan which sucks cold air into the engine compartment and blows it over the engine. This is known as air cooling. The generator can also be driven by

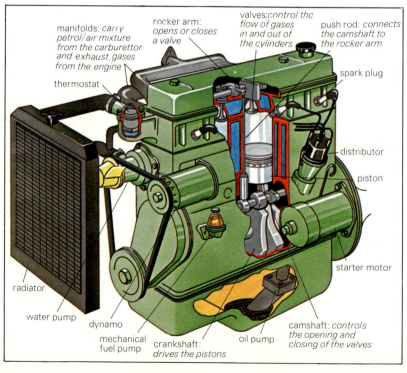

manifolds: *carry petrol/air mixture from the carburettor and exhaust gases from the engine*

rocker arm: *opens or closes a valve*

valves: *control the flow of gases in and out of the cylinders*

push rod: *connects the camshaft to the rocker arm*

thermostat

spark plug

distributor

piston

starter motor

radiator

water pump

dynamo

mechanical fuel pump

crankshaft: *drives the pistons*

oil pump

camshaft: *controls the opening and closing of the valves*

a pulley to make electricity to be stored in the battery. The generator, or dynamo provides D.C. or direct current like that of a torch battery. More and more cars are now using an alternator which provides A.C. or alternating current, such as ordinary household electricity, which is a more efficient system.

At the opposite end of the camshaft to the drive from the crankshaft is the oil pump which forces oil through the engine. The faster the engine runs the faster the oil pump turns and the higher the oil pressure becomes within the engine. Oil is extremely necessary to lubricate all the moving parts in the engine and gearbox, and if parts become worn, or oil is lost from the engine the oil pressure is reduced meaning that the oil cannot reach all the areas of the engine. If oil is lost from the engine, the moving parts become extremely hot due to friction

*Left:* The main parts of a motor car engine.
*Below:* The four-stroke cycle. Each stroke of the piston completes one stage of the cycle.

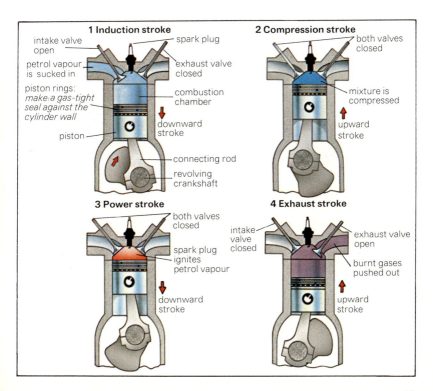

**1 Induction stroke**
intake valve open
spark plug
petrol vapour is sucked in
exhaust valve closed
combustion chamber
piston rings: *make a gas-tight seal against the cylinder wall*
piston
downward stroke
connecting rod
revolving crankshaft

**2 Compression stroke**
both valves closed
mixture is compressed
upward stroke

**3 Power stroke**
both valves closed
spark plug ignites petrol vapour
downward stroke

**4 Exhaust stroke**
intake valve closed
exhaust valve open
burnt gases pushed out
upward stroke

and can weld together or break up, causing much damage. It is therefore essential for a motorist to check both the oil pressure and the amount of oil present. A rod called the dipstick can be withdrawn from the engine to gauge the amount of oil present. Fresh oil can be poured into the engine by undoing a cap, usually in the rocker cover on top of the engine.

Most cars have engines of four or six cylinders but some more powerful engines have eight or twelve cylinders. Cylinders can be grouped in three ways: in-line, where the cylinders are one behind the other; v-shaped, where the crankshaft is at the base of the v and the pistons travel up and down on both sides of the crankshaft at an angle to each other; and thirdly horizontally where the crankshaft is between two sets of pistons which travel horizontally. Powerful racing engines are quite often of this type. The engine may be placed at the front of the car, at the rear of the car behind the rear wheels, or in a midway position just in front of the rear wheels. The engine may also point towards the front of the car or be in a transverse position, pointing from side to side.

**Fuel system**

The fuel used to power most cars is petrol. The liquid is stored in a tank and is pumped to the carburettor which mixes the petrol with air; this produces the inflammable vapour which is exploded in the top of the cylinder (the part known as the

air cleaner: *prevents dust entering the engine*

carburettor

intake manifold

fresh air sucked in

fuel tank

electric fuel pump

combustion chamber) by the sparking plug. Air enters the carburettor through the choke tube. Inside the choke is a valve which can restrict the amount of air coming in when the choke knob on the dashboard is pulled out. This helps to start the engine on cold mornings. Some cars have automatic chokes. Some high performance cars have fuel injection, which is an electronic system of metering the exact amount of fuel required by each cylinder.

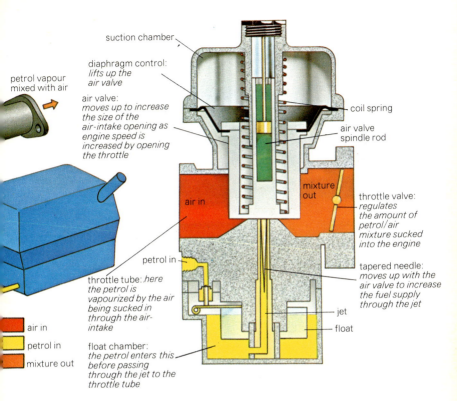

suction chamber

diaphragm control:
*lifts up the
air valve*

petrol vapour
mixed with air

air valve:
*moves up to increase
the size of the
air-intake opening as
engine speed is
increased by opening
the throttle*

coil spring

air valve
spindle rod

air in

mixture
out

throttle valve:
*regulates
the amount of
petrol/air
mixture sucked
into the engine*

petrol in

tapered needle:
*moves up with the
air valve to increase
the fuel supply
through the jet*

throttle tube: *here
the petrol is
vapourized by the air
being sucked in
through the air-
intake*

jet

float

air in

petrol in

mixture out

float chamber:
*the petrol enters this
before passing
through the jet to the
throttle tube*

*Left:* In the fuel system, petrol flows from the tank, through the pump to the carburettor, and then, as petrol vapour, through the manifolds to the cylinders. *Right:* In the carburettor, petrol is mixed with air as it is sprayed out of the jet, so that petrol vapour is formed.

One other control has an important bearing on the amount of fuel entering the engine, and that is the throttle or accelerator. When the driver places his foot on the accelerator he is allowing more of the air and petrol mixture to enter the engine, causing a larger explosion in the cylinders, and the car goes faster as a direct result.

**Ignition system**

As the fuel enters each of the four cylinders in turn it is exploded by the action of a sparking plug. This action is controlled by the distributor, which conveys an electric current to each of the sparking plugs in turn. This is accomplished by means of a rotor arm in the

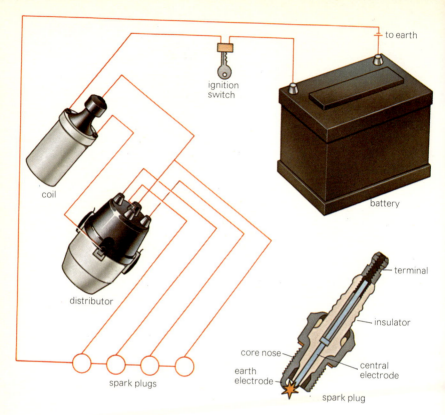

to earth

ignition
switch

coil

battery

distributor

terminal

insulator

core nose

central
electrode

earth
electrode

spark plug

spark plugs

distributor which revolves, making an electrical connection to each sparking plug in sequence. The movement of the rotor arm is activated by the camshaft through a special arrangement of gears.

Power for the ignition system is supplied from the battery. When the ignition is switched on an electric current flows from the battery to the coil. The coil converts the low voltage (tension) current from the battery (usually 12 volts) to a high voltage (tension) of several thousand

In the ignition system, power from the battery flows to the spark plugs, via the distributor and coil, when the engine is started.

volts. From the coil the power flows to the distributor and thence to the sparking plugs.

**Diesel engine**

The diesel engine is similar to its forerunner the petrol engine in many respects. The main difference is that the petrol engine works by spark ignition and the diesel engine works by compression ignition. The

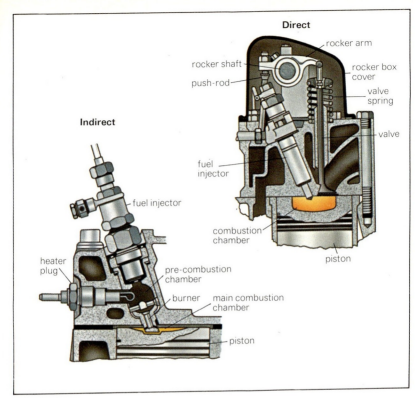

**Direct**

rocker arm

rocker shaft

rocker box cover

push-rod

valve spring

**Indirect**

valve

fuel injector

fuel injector

combustion chamber

heater plug

pre-combustion chamber

piston

burner

main combustion chamber

piston

operation of compression ignition engines is based on the fact that when air is compressed, heat is developed (you might have noticed when using a bicycle tyre pump that as the pressure increases inside the tyre more effort is needed to operate the pump, and the barrel of the pump becomes hotter and hotter). In the diesel engine the air is compressed until high temperatures are reached, then the diesel oil is pumped or injected into the engine where the hot air ignites it, causing

The diesel ignition system involves fuel injection, which can be either indirect (left) or direct (right).

the power explosion. Diesel engines are simpler than petrol engines as there is no electrical system needed to ignite the fuel.

The 4-stroke diesel cycle works as follows: 1. *Induction stroke:* clean air is sucked into the cylinders through valves, as the piston is moving downwards. 2. *Compression stroke:* the intake valve closes and all the air in

63

the cylinder is compressed as the piston rises. The temperature of the air rises quickly to a greater heat than that required to ignite the fuel, which is injected just before the piston reaches the top of its stroke. 3. *Power stroke:* the high temperature due to the burning diesel causes the combustion gases to expand. This forces the piston downwards providing the motive force for the wheels. 4. *Exhaust stroke:* the exhaust valve opens and the burnt gases are pushed out of the cylinder as the piston rises once more.

## Transmission

It is obviously necessary to have some means of disconnecting the engine from the wheels, or it would not be possible for the car to remain stationary with the engine still running, or to change gear. This is accomplished by means of the clutch. To change from one gear to another the driver first pushes his foot down on the clutch pedal. This releases the pressure plate in the clutch and allows the friction plate to run free so that the engine is disconnected from the gearbox. Once the gear is selected, the driver lifts his foot off the clutch pedal, which re-engages the drive between the engine and the road wheels.

Whilst the gear selected determines the speed of the car this is also affected by the amount of petrol and air being fed to the engine by the accelerator.

From the gearbox the power is transmitted to the road wheels. A system of gears, known as the differential, allows for the fact that the outer wheels have to travel faster than the inner wheels when the vehicle is cornering.

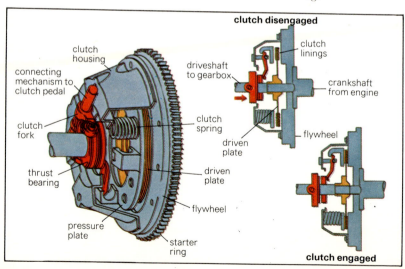

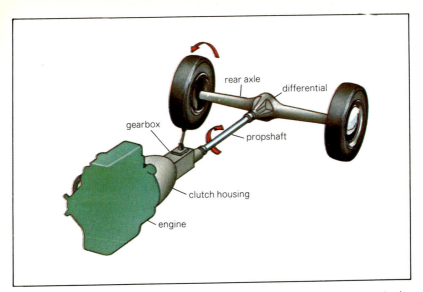

rear axle

differential

gearbox

propshaft

clutch housing

engine

*Below left:* The clutch disengages the engine from the gearbox, making it possible to change from one gear to another. *Right:* From the gearbox, the power is transmitted to the road wheels via the propshaft and axle.

There are two types of clutch – the friction clutch and the fluid clutch. The friction clutch consists of sprung metal plates. Part of the clutch is connected to the flywheel and part is connected to a shaft, called the transmission shaft, that leads to the gearbox. When the driver pushes his foot on the clutch pedal these plates are separated so that the drive is not transmitted through the clutch and gearbox to the road wheels. As the clutch pedal is released the plates move back together so that the power is once again transmitted from the engine to the wheels.

The fluid clutch is used in automatic transmission. Attached to the end of the shaft from the engine is a bowl containing a fan-like structure. Next to it, at the end of the shaft leading to the flywheel, is another fan. The space between the two is filled with oil. When the fan connected to the engine turns it moves the oil which causes the fan on the propellor shaft to rotate. Because there is no physical contact between the transmission shaft and the propshaft or driveshafts there is no need to disengage the clutch to change gear.

The gearbox consists of a series of different-sized gears, and by moving the gearstick the driver causes different sets of gears to enmesh with each other. This has the effect of changing the speed of the propshaft or driveshafts, and hence the speed of the road wheels. The purpose of the gearbox is to alter the speed at which the car is driven, so that even if the engine is turning at a constant speed, the speed at which the road wheels turn will be altered.

Such a device is necessary because the internal combustion engine works most efficiently when it is turning at a relatively high number of revolutions. This is fine for driving the car at speed, but with just one gear the car would not be able to climb hills effectively or slow down for corners. The gears enable this to be done whilst still retaining the same power output from the engine. When running at speed on a level road the driver is able to make full use of the engine potential by choosing the highest of the gears that are available to him.

Most cars have four gears, but some have five. The lowest of these, which gives the lowest speed, is used for starting and for hill climbing, and is known as first gear. The speed produced by the second and third gears increases progressively, and the fourth, or top gear, is used for high-speed cruising. In addition to the forward gears there is also a reverse gear which enables the car to move backwards.

The parts that make up a cross-ply tyre, showing how the plies are arranged.

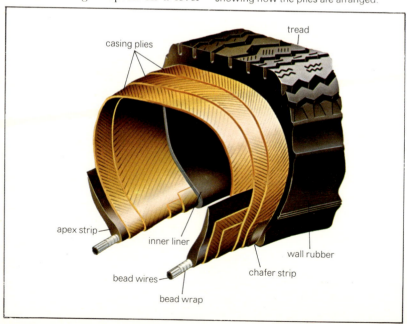

casing plies

tread

apex strip

inner liner

bead wires

bead wrap

chafer strip

wall rubber

# Tyres

The law requires that all tyres must be pneumatic (filled with air), and must be inflated to the correct pressure as set out in the figures issued by the tyre manufacturers. All tyres fitted to a vehicle must be in good condition. To fit defective or worn tyres is not only dangerous, it is also against the law. The tread pattern must be at least one millimetre in depth for at least three quarters of the tread width, all the way round the tyre.

There are two main types of tyre used in Europe: cross-ply and radial-ply. The fabric layers of a cross-ply tyre are arranged so that the cords run at an oblique angle to the bead (the edge of the tyre). The layers are arranged so that the cords in each layer cross one another. This imparts additional rigidity to the tyre.

In a radial-ply tyre the cords are arranged at right angles to the bead so that they run from one side of the tyre to the other. This follows the line of a radius drawn from the centre of the tyre, and is the reason why such tyres are called radials. The arrangement of the cords gives great suppleness to the tyre walls, but it is necessary to reinforce the tread area with a number of

In a radial tyre the cords run from one side of the tyre to the other.

tread bracing layers

tread

radial plies

inner liner

bead wrap

bead wires

apex strip

chafer strip

wall rubber

additional layers of fabric or steel. This forms a tyre that has flexible walls to absorb vehicle movement but a flat tread to provide maximum contact with the road surface. Radial tyres are becoming increasingly popular, and it is envisaged that the day is not far off when their use will be almost universal.

In recent years the failsafe tyre has made its appearance. This type of tyre is designed so that should a puncture occur, the car can continue to be run for a considerable period. When an ordinary tubeless tyre goes flat it rolls itself off the rim of the wheel. The wheel rims and the beads of a failsafe tyre are so constructed that the tyre is not shed from the rim after a puncture. Another safety built into the failsafe tyre is an amount of liquid lubricant. When a tyre is punctured this lubricant is released and prevents the tyre wall from burning up as a result of friction. The lubricant also helps to seal the puncture.

## Stopping distances

Something that all road users, not just motorists, should bear in mind at all times is the distance required for a car to stop. An average family saloon travelling at 48 kilometres per hour (30 miles per hour) on a dry road will, provided the driver is alert and the car has good brakes, take in the region of 23 metres (75 feet) between the time that the driver spots an emergency and the time that the car comes to a halt. In such an instance the car has probably travelled somewhere in the region of 9 metres (30 feet) before the driver even reacts to the situation.

Some other stopping distances, together with the distance covered before the driver reacts are given here. It should be remembered, however, that these reflect ideal circumstances. If the brakes are not as good as they should be, if the driver is tired, or if the road is wet or slippery these distances could be lengthened quite considerably.

This diagram shows the shortest stopping distance for each speed, but under less-than-ideal conditions these distances may be longer.

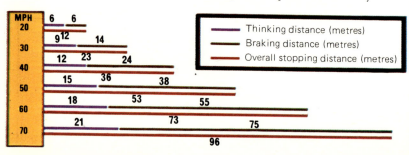

| MPH | | |
|---|---|---|
| 20 | 6 | 6 |
| 30 | 9 12 | 14 |
| 40 | 12 23 | 24 |
| 50 | 15 36 | 38 |
| 60 | 18 53 | 55 |
| 70 | 21 73 | 75 |
| | 96 | |

Thinking distance (metres)
Braking distance (metres)
Overall stopping distance (metres)

# Technical terms

There are many words which have a special meaning to motorists and other road users: here are brief explanations of some of them.

**Additive** Chemical that can be added to petrol or oil to improve performance, or reduce engine wear.

**Alternator** A generator that produces a rapidly alternating current (flowing first in one and then the opposite direction).

**Antifreeze** Chemical added to the cooling system during cold weather to prevent the water from freezing.

**Anti-roll bar** A steel bar linking one side of the chassis with the other. It helps to balance out movement of the suspension and lessens the tendency to roll onto the side.

**Anti-theft lock** Fitted as a standard item on many cars, this device locks the steering when the ignition key is removed.

**Aquaplaning** When the tread of the tyres cannot push away water on the road it builds up beneath them until the car is riding on a film of water, and controlling the vehicle becomes impossible.

**Backfire** A premature explosion in the engine or exhaust system, usually caused by incorrect ignition timing.

**Bhp** Brake horse power; a unit for the measurement of the power produced by an engine.

**Camshaft** Revolving shaft within the engine of a vehicle which, by means of projections along its length, opens the inlet and exhaust valves for each cylinder.

**Carburettor** Device for mixing petrol with air to provide fuel for the engine.

**CC** Cubic centimetres; the cubic capacity of all the cylinders.

**Choke** Device that reduces the amount of air entering the carburettor so that a richer petrol mixture enters the engine. Operated by the driver with a lever on or beneath the dashboard.

**Clutch** Mechanism that disconnects and connects the drive between the engine and the wheels.

**Coil** An electrical component which converts low-voltage electricity supplied from the battery, to brief bursts of high-voltage electricity at exact intervals of time.

**Compression ratio** The figure obtained by comparing the volume above a piston at the bottom of its stroke with that at the top of its stroke.

**Crankshaft** Shaft connected by rods to the pistons, that converts their reciprocating (up and down) action into rotary motion.

**Cross-ply tyre** Tyre in which the cords are set at an oblique angle to the rim.

**Cylinder** The part of the engine in which a piston moves up and down.

**Dashboard** The driver's instrument panel, sometimes abbreviated to 'dash'; sometimes called fascia.

**Demister** Device that directs hot air on to the windscreen to clear condensation or frost.

69

**Differential** Mechanical system that transmits power from the propshaft or the driveshafts to the driving wheels, whilst allowing the outer driving wheel to turn faster than the inner wheel when turning a corner.

**Dip stick** Metal rod which is inserted in the sump and which provides an indication of the oil level.

**Distributor** High-voltage electricity from the coil is fed into the distributor by the central wire in the distributor cap. The electricity passes through a revolving, or rotor, arm and causes a spark to be passed to the terminals of leads which distribute the electricity to the sparking plugs.

**Fuel consumption** The distance a car can travel on a given amount of fuel. Usually quoted as miles per gallon (mpg) or kilometres per litre (kpl).

**GT** Abbreviation of Gran Turismo (Grand Touring), generally meaning a fast luxury coupé for two people with enough space for basic luggage. Nowadays misapplied to many cars.

**Independent suspension** Used to describe vehicles that have individual springing on each of the four wheels.

**Jack** Device used to raise part of the car off the ground.

**Kerb weight** The weight of a vehicle with half a tank of petrol.

**Odometer** Device that registers, on a dial or meter on the dashboard, the distance covered by the vehicle.

**Rack and pinion** Type of steering system. A small gear at the base of the steering column moves a toothed rod from one side to the other to steer the wheels.

**Radial-ply tyre** Tyre in which the cords are set at right angles to the rim.

**Shock absorber** The part of the suspension used to dampen down body movement to prevent too much wear on the suspension, and to prevent the vehicle from bouncing along bumpy roads.

**Synchromesh** Diagonal teeth on gear wheels in the gearbox allowing the gears to be changed with ease.

**Tachometer** Device on the dashboard that indicates the number of revolutions made by the crankshaft each minute. Also known as rev. (revolution) counter.

**Thermostat** Device in the cooling system which prevents water from returning to the radiator until the engine has warmed up.

**Torque** The amount of power that has to be produced by the pistons to turn the crankshaft.

**Transmission** The system that conveys the power (torque) produced by the pistons to the driving wheels.

**Trip recorder** Odometer that can be set at zero at the start of each journey.

**Turning circle** The circle described by a vehicle when the steering wheel is on full lock (turned to its furthest extent).

# Places to Visit

## Looking at churches

As you travel around the country you will pass many old churches. There are over 16,000 parish churches in British villages and towns, and the church warrants special interest for it is invariably the oldest building in the community. It is possible to get some idea of a church's age just by looking at its style of architecture as you pass by on the road. You do not have to be an expert to gain a lot of pleasure from looking at old churches, and the pictorial guide will give you a useful start.

The basic forms of English churches are shown below

## Saxon churches

The majority of churches built prior to 1066 were made of timber, and the oldest survivor is the Church of St Andrew at Greensted-Juxta-Ongar, Essex. Built from solid oak, it is known to date from at least 1013 and tests have shown that it could have been built as far back as A.D. 850.

Towards the end of the Saxon Period the importance of the church increased and stone became the usual building material. The towers of such churches are invariably square, with extremely thick walls and very small windows and doors. The stones at the corners of the tower are arranged alternately horizontal and vertical.

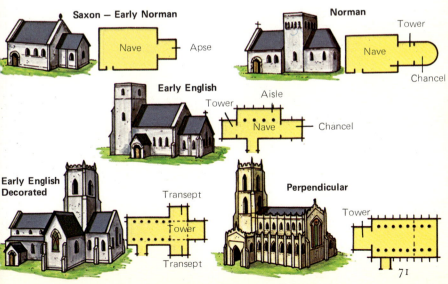

**Saxon – Early Norman**
Nave — Apse

**Norman**
Tower
Nave
Chancel

**Early English**
Tower — Nave — Aisle — Chancel

**Early English Decorated**
Transept — Tower — Transept

**Perpendicular**
Tower

71

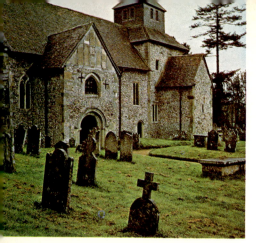

## Norman churches

Churches with semicircular arches to their doors and windows, and with square towers, are generally Norman in origin. This style of church was built from 1066 to the end of the twelfth century. Other clues to look for are the plain buttresses (the supports at the sides of the church), and the stones at the corners of the tower which are arranged in the same fashion as those of a Saxon church. If you go inside you will find that the columns

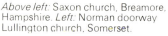

*Above left:* Saxon church, Breamore, Hampshire. *Left:* Norman doorway Lullington church, Somerset.

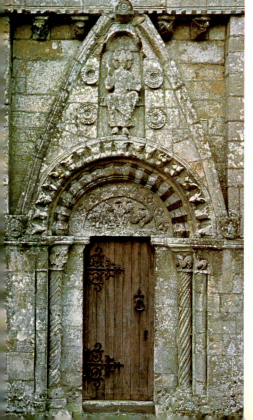

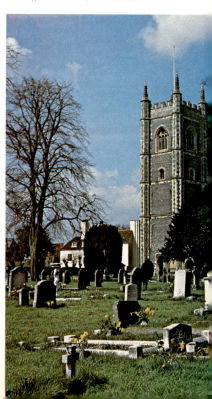

of Norman churches are solid and simple with square capitals. A capital is the top part of a pillar, usually wider at the top than the column which supports it.

## Early English churches

A hundred years after the Norman Conquest the square tower was still a feature of the church, but the windows and doors consist of pointed arches. The buttresses are still fairly simple in design but are often built in two stages and are sloped at the top. This type of

*Below:* A Perpendicular church, to be seen at Dedham, Essex.

church, sometimes known as 'Gothic' was built from about 1160 to the early thirteenth century.

## Decorated churches

In the fourteenth century the church became much more decorative in style. The tower is more elaborate than those of previous years and possesses a steeple, often eight sided. On the external walls gargoyles and other carvings are well in evidence. The buttresses are very ornate as are the windows with their mullions (vertical columns between window panes) and delicate tracery. The doors, too, are often richly carved. Contrasting with all this finery are the pillars to be found in this type of church, for they have a classic simplicity all of their own.

## Perpendicular churches

Fifteenth-century churches were built in what is known as 'perpendicular style'. The emphasis of the design and decoration in such churches is often towards the vertical line, the windows being divided into many smaller windows to provide the perpendicular effect. This is carried through to the door, of which the arch is flattened or depressed, and also to the buttresses which give the appearance of having been panelled.

## Renaissance churches

From the sixteenth to the nineteenth century churches were often built in the style of Greek and Roman temples. A feature of such churches is the classical style columns used both inside the building and on the exterior. During this period many architects continued to prefer the old Gothic style, and many churches were built in the old style.

There are many clues, in addition to the ones given here, that will tell you the age of a church. You will also find that a great number of churches contain a number of different styles as each generation added to or restored the building.

## Looking at castles

The word 'castle' usually refers to fortresses built after the Norman Conquest. There are, however, many fortresses and defence works built before this date. Several of the older fortresses consisted of tremendous earthworks, and traces of these can be found all over the country. It is easier still to find remains of Roman defence works, the most notable being Hadrian's Wall that runs from coast to coast across the top of England. In fact, our word 'castle' comes from the Latin 'castellum', meaning a small fortress.

The first true castles in the British Isles were built prior to the Battle of Hastings (1066). They are of the *motte and bailey* type, as were those built after the Conquest until about 1100. Over a hundred castles of this type were built in Britain. The motte was a mound of earth on top of which was a timber building. Surrounding the motte there was usually a ditch filled with sharpened

sticks or water (hence our word 'moat'). This ditch was dug out for defence but also to provide the earth that made up the motte.

Surrounding the motte was an outer ditch and mound, on top of which was a wooden stockade. The courtyard enclosed by this wall was called the bailey. Sometimes there was both an outer and an inner bailey.

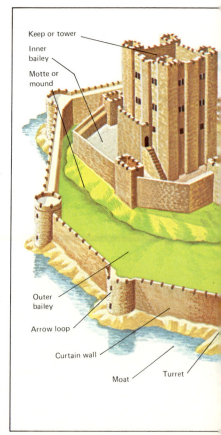

Keep or tower
Inner bailey
Motte or mound
Outer bailey
Arrow loop
Curtain wall
Moat
Turret

At Thetford in Norfolk there is a mound of earth some 24 metres (79 feet high). It was once the motte of an eleventh century motte and bailey castle and is the highest mound of its type in Britain. A motte and bailey castle can also be seen at Berkhamsted, Hertfordshire. This had stone buildings added to it in later generations, but it was originally built in Norman times.

Unfortunately, very little of it remains. The impressive castles at Durham, Warwick and Windsor were originally motte and bailey castles of earth and timber construction which were later extended.

The next stage in the development of British castles was the building of great stone towers, or keeps, during the first half of the twelfth

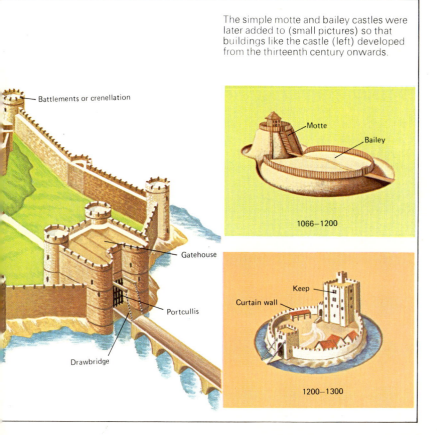

The simple motte and bailey castles were later added to (small pictures) so that buildings like the castle (left) developed from the thirteenth century onwards.

Battlements or crenellation

Gatehouse

Portcullis

Drawbridge

Motte

Bailey

1066–1200

Keep

Curtain wall

1200–1300

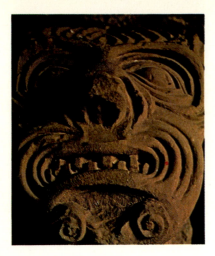

Gargoyles, such as this one at Caerlaverock castle, were spouts, carrying off rainwater from the gutters. Here, the water comes out of the nose.

towers were built, and a rampart walk was added to the top of the walls so that the defenders could prevent anyone from climbing up. At first the towers were square but these proved too vulnerable to attacks by battering ram and cannon, and so later castles were built with circular towers. By this time the overall design of the castle had changed quite considerably. They now consisted of several strong walls situated one inside the other, each wall being extremely strong and well equipped to ward off attacks. This type of castle is known as a *concentric castle*, a particularly fine example of which can be seen at Beaumaris on Anglesey, North Wales. The best surviving example in Scotland is Caerlaverock Castle in Dumfries and Galloway.

By the sixteenth century the era of great castles was at an end. This was due partly to the increasing use of gunpowder and partly to the more settled conditions within the country itself. Building of private castles was, in any case, prohibited by law as a safeguard against the possibility of internal rebellion. The closest resemblance to a castle that the lesser gentry could now have was a fortified manor house.

Most of the castles that you will see on your travels will probably

century. The keep was surrounded by a stone wall which was in turn protected by an outer wall, also of stone. In the thirteenth century the walls were crenellated – indented with the tooth like structures that one usually associates with castles. This was a defensive technique learned from studying castles in the Middle East during the Crusades; a soldier could duck behind the raised part of the wall after firing an arrow through the lower part. The castle was further protected about this time by the introduction of a grill – the portcullis – to secure the main gate (the weakest part of the castle's defences).

At intervals around the wall,

*Above right:* Windsor Castle, Berkshire.
*Right:* Caerlaverock Castle, Dumfries and Galloway.

contain several different styles fused together as each successive generation added improvements to an existing site. Windsor, for example, England's biggest castle, was originally a motte and bailey. This has been improved and enlarged through the centuries. Pevensey Castle was built on the site of a Roman fort. An inner wall and moat were added in the thirteenth century and improvements have been added almost up to the present day. It was last fortified in 1945, being used as a defensive position in the Second World War.

Arundel Castle, Sussex.

# Major castles of the United Kingdom

## England

*Arundel Castle*, Sussex (on A27, north of Littlehampton). Norman castle much restored. Home of the Duke of Norfolk.

*Bamburgh Castle*, Northumberland (on B1342 east of Farne Islands). Norman castle, scene of fierce fighting during the Wars of the Roses.

*Belvoir Castle*, Leicestershire (west of Grantham, between A52 and A607). On hilltop overlooking Vale of Belvoir. Contains a magnificent private art collection.

*Berkeley Castle*, Gloucestershire (on B4509 midway between Gloucester and Bristol). Scene of the murder of King Edward II in 1327.

*Bodiam Castle*, Sussex (south-east from Hawkhurst between A229 and A268). Attractive moated castle built in 1386.

*Carlisle Castle*, Cumbria (at Carlisle). Twelfth century border fortress used by both Scottish and English forces.

*Colchester Castle*, Essex (at Colchester). One of the oldest stone castles in England.

*Conisbrough Castle*, Yorkshire (on A630 between Doncaster and Rotherham). Built late twelfth century with unusual six-buttressed circular keep.

*Deal Castle*, Kent (at Deal). Built by Henry VIII, between 1539 and 1541, as a coastal fortress.

*Dover Castle*, Kent (at Dover).

Impressive Norman building with Roman lighthouse nearby.

*Durham Castle*, Durham (at Durham). Imposing Norman castle, now part of Durham University, overlooking the town.

*Herstmonceaux Castle*, Sussex (south from A271, east of Hailsham). Beautiful fifteenth century building now the home of the Royal Greenwich Observatory. Only the grounds are open to the public.

*Ludlow Castle*, Salop (at Ludlow). Founded by Roger de Lacey in 1086, and added to at various times up to the sixteenth century.

*Pevensey Castle*, Sussex (at Pevensey between Eastbourne and Bexhill). Roman fort built in the third century with Norman and thirteenth century additions.

*Rochester Castle*, Kent (at Rochester). Norman castle besieged by King John in 1215. It has an impressive four-storeyed keep built 1123–36.

*Warwick Castle*, Warwickshire (at Warwick). Although much restored, this fourteenth century home of the Earls of Warwick is one of the most beautiful castles in England.

## Scotland

*Bothwell Castle*, Strathclyde (on A74 southeast of Glasgow). Impressive ruins of an ancient Scottish stronghold.

*Caerlaverock Castle*, Dumfries and Galloway (on B725 southeast of Dumfries). Medieval stronghold captured by Edward I in 1300.

*Crathes Castle*, Grampian (on A93 south-west of Aberdeen). Stands on land given by Robert the Bruce to the Burnett family in 1323. Famous for its painted ceilings and eighteenth century gardens.

*Dunvegan Castle*, Highland (on the Isle of Skye). Thirteenth century home of the Chief of the Macleods.

*Edinburgh Castle*, Lothian (at Edinburgh). Great and historic fortress that overlooks the Scottish capital. It was used by Scottish kings from the eleventh century.

## Wales

*Beaumaris Castle*, Gwynedd (at Beaumaris). Concentric castle built by Edward I and used as the Welsh administrative headquarters of the English government.

*Caernarvon Castle*, Gwynedd (at Caernarvon). Birthplace of Edward I in 1283. Prince Charles was invested as Prince of Wales here in 1969.

*Caerphilly Castle*, Glamorgan (on A470 north of Cardiff). The largest thirteenth century fortress in Wales. Famous for its leaning tower, the result of an attempt to blow it up in the Middle Ages.

*Cilgerran Castle*, Dyfed (between A478 and A484 4 miles south of Cardigan). Ruin of thirteenth and fourteenth century castle sited above the River Teifi.

*Conway Castle*, Gwynedd (at Conway). Triangular curtain wall with eight round towers built between 1283 and 1290.

*Harlech Castle*, Gwynedd (at Harlech). Built by Edward I, this castle was begun in 1283. The defence of the castle by Dafydd ab Einion in 1468 inspired the famous song 'Men of Harlech'.

*Pembroke Castle*, Dyfed (at Pembroke). Magnificent circular keep within a curtain wall. Birthplace of King Henry VII in 1457.

## Northern Ireland

*Antrim Castle*, (at Antrim). Ruined seventeenth century castle, once the home of the Massereene family.

*Dunluce Castle*, **Antrim (on A2 east of Portrush).** Fourteenth century

Although only the ruins of the fourteenth century castle remain at Dunluce, County Antrim, it is still an impressive sight.

stronghold atop a projecting rock, and connected to the mainland only by a narrow bridge.

*Dundrum Castle*, Down (off A24 north-east of Newcastle). Circular 13 metre (43 foot) high keep is one of the features of this twelfth century stronghold.

*Carrickfergus Castle*, Antrim (at Carrickfergus north-east of Belfast on A2). King William II landed here in 1690 prior to the Battle of the Boyne.

*Mountjoy Castle*, Tyrone (on B161 north-east of Dungannon). Built in 1602, this castle has walls 76cm (2½ feet) thick.

# Museums

During your journey why not visit a museum? Today, many museums are exciting places which have geared their displays to move with the times, and are no longer the dusty, gloomy places so often depicted. Although such places do still exist, this type of museum is now largely a thing of the past – a museum piece in its own right.

Many museums are in fact coming out of their shells completely and moving out into the open air. The concept of open air museums was born in Scandinavia at the turn of the century, but it was not until the 1950s that the idea really became popular in Britain, although the Manx Open Air Museum at Cregneash on the Isle of Man and the Highland Folk Museum at Kingussie in Scotland had been open for more than a decade by that time.

Cregneash contains part of a Celtic farming community consisting of nine stone buildings preserved and restored in their original setting.

Ironbridge Gorge Museum is a unique tribute to Britain's industrial revolution, and is in Coalbrookdale, Shropshire.

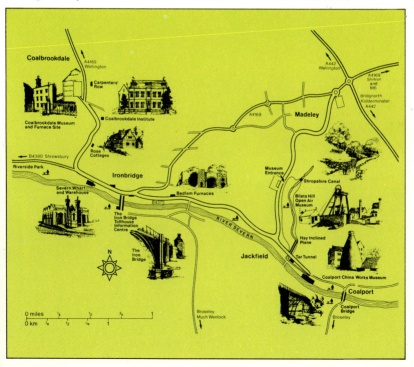

These include a blacksmith's shop, a crofter's cottage, a weaver's shed, and the outbuildings of a farmstead. And to make the scene even more realistic there is also a flock of Manx brown sheep to greet the visitor.

Whereas the settlement at Cregneash is displayed on its original site, the buildings at Kingussie have been recreated on a special museum site. There is still a great deal of argument between the experts as to which is the most effective method of display. The grounds at Kingussie contain a fully furnished, full-scale replica of a farm cottage complete with a mill and a dairy shed.

Possibly the best-known of the

Open Air Museums in England is the Ironbridge Gorge Museum which was opened in 1968. Ironbridge, so named because this part of Coalbrookdale boasts the world's first iron bridge which still spans the River Severn as it has since 1779, is a unique and impressive monument to our industrial heritage. It was at Coalbrookdale in 1709 that Abraham Darby started a revolution in iron smelting by utilising coke instead of charcoal in the process, a technical breakthrough that made possible the extensive use of cast iron. In addition to the first iron bridge, this iron-orientated community was also responsible for building the first iron boat and the world's first steam railway locomotive.

This bridge gave the nearby village of Ironbridge, Shropshire, its name.

A replica of Stephenson's 'Locomotion' to be seen at the North of England Open Air Museum, Beamish.

Further north, at Beamish in County Durham, there is another open air museum dedicated to showing the heyday of British industrial development and how people lived and worked in England during the last century. The task of collecting the many thousands of items needed for such a project has been going on for several years and is still not complete. It is intended that the museum will eventually house a complete town with cobbled streets and shops, as well as a village with a blacksmith's shop and village post office. Other parts of the museum are being devoted to the development of industry, transport, and leisure. Many of these projects have not yet been started, although others are under way, but there is already a great deal to see and delight the visitor. It is even possible to take a ride on an old tram that used to operate for Gateshead Tramways early this century.

If you like travelling on trams or indeed any other form of transport, then you may like to visit one of the special museums that deal exclusively with transport. At Dinting Railway Centre, for example, it is possible to take a footplate ride on a steam locomotive. Many engines, both main line and shunting, are on view daily but to see them operating you must go on a Sunday or a Bank Holiday. If you like aircraft, try the R.A.F. Museum at Hendon in London where you can see some forty aeroplanes in addition to several general galleries devoted to aviation. Or perhaps you prefer tanks? Then how about the Royal Armoured Corps Tank Museum at Bovingdon Camp at Wareham in Dorset where you can see over a hundred armoured fighting vehicles dating from 1915.

In fact whatever special interest you have, you can be almost certain that there is a museum somewhere that caters for your taste. In Newcastle-upon-Tyne you will find a museum devoted to bagpipes, and there are many other musical museums around the country including the Russell Collection of Harpsichords and Clavichords in Edinburgh. Also in Edinburgh there is a Museum of Childhood which covers all types of children's toys, games, books and so on. Another museum of childhood can be found at Menai Bridge on Anglesey, not a stone's throw from the bridge itself.

## Museum guide

A few open air specialist museums that will be of interest are given below, together with brief details of what they contain.

## Open-air museums

### England

*Abbeydale Industrial Hamlet*, Abbeydale Road South, Sheffield, Yorkshire (Tel: Sheffield 367731). An eighteenth-century steel and scytheworks including forges, tilt-hammers, steel furnace and workmen's cottages.

*Abbot's Hall Museum of Rural Life of East Anglia*, Stowmarket, Suffolk (Tel: Stowmarket 2229). Agricultural implements and household goods. A fourteenth-century 'aisled-hall' farmhouse, smithy and sixteenth-century barn.

*Ironbridge Gorge Museum Trust*, Church Hill, Ironbridge, Telford, Salop (Tel: Ironbridge 3522). Unique collection of monuments relating to the industrial revolution including steam-blowing engines, and furnaces on two sites.

*Manx Open Air Museum*, Cregneash, Isle of Man (Tel. Douglas 5522). Stone buildings, mostly thatched, including a crofter's cottage, smithy and farm buildings; also sheep.

*North of England Open Air Museum*, Beamish, Nr Stanley, Durham (Tel: Stanley 33586). Estate buildings, railway station, 1925 electric tram, 100-tonne steam 'navvy' excavator, farm cottages, Victorian pub.

*Ryedale Folk Museum*, Hutton-le-Hole, Yorkshire (Tel: Lastingham 367). Implements, domestic appliances and furniture reflecting the life and work of an agricultural community.

*Weald and Downland Open Air Museum*, Singleton, Nr Chichester, Sussex (Tel: Singleton 348). Historic buildings from south-east England including an Elizabethan tread mill, an eighteenth-century market granary, and reconstructions of a Saxon weaver's hut and a charcoal burner's camp. Woodland nature trail and attractive picnic areas.

## Scotland

*Argyll Museum of Farming Life*, Auchindrain, Strathclyde (Tel: Fur-

An old loom at the Esgair Moel woollen mill at the Welsh Folk Museum.

ance 235). A joint-tenure farm comprising byre houses, stable and a smithy; also shetland ponies, Jacob's sheep and Highland cattle.

*Highland Folk Museum*, Kingussie, Highland (Tel: Kingussie 307). Collection of Highland antiquities including examples of crafts and tartans, furnished cottage, mill and dairy shed.

## Wales

*Welsh Folk Museum*, St Fagans, Nr Cardiff, Glamorgan (Tel: Cardiff 561357/8). St Fagans castle, farmhouses, tannery, cock-fighting pit, and other folk life exhibits; also a flock of sheep.

## Northern Ireland

*Ulster Folk Museum*, Cultra Manor, Holywood, Down BT18 OEU (Tel: Holywood 3555-9). Indoor and outdoor exhibition of material relating to the traditional life of Ulster.

---

## Specialist museums

### England

*America* The American Museum, Claverton Manor, Nr Bath, Avon (Tel: Bath 60503). Eighteen furnished period rooms and galleries of special exhibits. A special section is devoted to the American Indian.

*Bagpipes* The Bagpipe Museum, The Black Gate, St Nicholas Street, Newcastle-upon-Tyne, Tyne and Wear. Wide-ranging collection of bagpipes and pipe music recordings.

*Buildings* Avoncroft Museum of

Gentleman's slipper
c.1660-80

Lady's shoe
c.1765

Lady's boot
c.1865

Gentleman's boot
c.1875

Some of the shoes to be seen at the Street Shoe Museum.

Lady's velvet shoe
c.1660

Lady's boot
c.1840

Girl's shoe
1856

Lady's shoe,
Paris c.1895

Buildings, Stoke Heath, Broms-grove, Hereford and Worcester B60 4JR. Buildings from the Iron Age to the eighteenth century including Danzy Green post-mill, and a fifteenth-century merchant's house.

*Cars and motor cycles* National Motor Museum, Palace House, Beaulieu, Hampshire (Tel: Beaulieu 612345). Veteran and vintage cars, commercial vehicles and motor cycles.

*Glass* The Pilkington Glass Museum, Pilkington Brothers Ltd, Prescot Road, St Helen's, Merseyside (Tel: St Helen's 2882 extn. 2499). History and development of glass making.

*Maritime* Exeter Maritime Museum, The Quay, Exeter, Devon (Tel: Exeter 58075). Working craft from all over the world, many of which are afloat and can be explored freely. Launch trips in summer, weather permitting.

*Pipes* House of Pipes, Bramber, Sussex (Tel: Steyning 812122). Unique collection of pipes and smoking paraphernalia from all over the world.

*Railways* National Railway Museum, Leeman Road, York, Yorkshire (Tel: York 21261). Exhibits covering the history and development of British railway engineering. Famous locomotives, rolling stock, railway equipment, pictures and working models.

*Railways* Dinting Railway Centre, Dinting Lane, Glossop, Derbyshire (Tel: Glossop 5596). Main-line steam engines (Bahamas, Leander, Cheltenham classes, etc.) and shunting locomotives housed in a ten-acre steam-operating depot. Engines operating on Sundays and Bank Holidays.

*Shoes* Street Shoe Museum, C. & J. Clark Ltd, High Street, Street, Somerset (Tel: Street 43131). Shoes from Roman times to the twentieth century, shoe machinery, and documents and photographs relating to the company.

*Trams* The Tramway Museum, Matlock Road, Crich, Nr Matlock, Derbyshire (Tel: Ambergate 2565). Horse, steam and electric trams.

*Transport* The Shuttleworth Collection, Old Warden Aerodrome, Biggleswade, Bedfordshire (Tel: Northill 288). Aeroplanes, cars, carriages, bicycles and fire engines, many of which are in working order.

## Scotland

*Childhood* Museum of Childhood, 38 High Street, Edinburgh, Scotland (Tel: 031-556-5447). Games, toys, costume and educational exhibits connected with children.

## Wales

*Slate Quarrying* North Wales Quarrying Museum, Llanberis, Gwyned (Tel: Llanberis 630). Machinery and equipment connected with slate quarrying. Demonstrations of slate splitting and dressing.

## Eire

*Brewing* The Guinness Museum, Arthur Guinness, Son and Co (Dublin) Ltd, Watling Street, Dublin, Eire. Cooper's tools, brewing equipment, transportation, advertising and brewing in Ireland.

# On safari

The map on the opposite page shows some of the many safari parks and animal reserves that can be visited in Britain.

## England

*Curraghs Wildlife Park*, Bellaugh, Isle of Man. Pumas, llamas, monkeys, flamingoes and penguins.

*Knowsley Safari Park*, Prescot, Lancashire. Lions, zebras, giraffes, elephants, monkeys, antelopes, white rhinoceroses, camels and cheetahs.

*Lampton Lion Park*, Chester-le-Street, Durham. Lions, zebras, giraffes, baboons and birds.

*Lions of Longleat*, Longleat, Warminster, Wiltshire. Lions, giraffes, chimpanzees, hippopotamuses, sea lions, **tigers, elephants, camels, rhinoceroses, cheetahs, and boat safari.**

*Stapleford Lion Reserve*, Stapleford, Melton Mowbray, Leicestershire. Lions, leopards, monkeys, crocodiles, bears and deer.

*Suffolk Wildlife and Country Park*, Kessingland, Nr Lowestoft, Suffolk. Lions, pumas, tigers, timber wolves, wallabies, deer and monkeys.

*Thorney Wildlife Park*, Thorney, Peterborough, Northamptonshire. Lions, leopards, giraffes, llamas, pumas, elephants, tigers, panthers, wallabies, deer and monkeys.

*West Country Wildlife Park*, Cricket St Thomas, Chard, Somerset. Leopards, lynxes, pumas and monkeys.

*Right:* Where to find the safari parks of Britain.

1 Scotland's African Safari Park

2 Loch Lomond Bear Park

3 Causeway Safari Park

4 Lampton Lion Park

5 Curraghs Wildlife Park

6 Knowsley Safari Park

7 Stapleford Lion Reserve

8 West Midland Safari Park

9 Thorney Wildlife Park

10 Suffolk Wildlife and Country Park

11 Woburn Wild Animal Kingdom

12 Whipsnade Park Zoo

13 Lions of Longleat

14 Windsor Safari Park

15 West Country Wildlife Park

*West Midland Safari Park*, Spring Grove, Bewdley, Hereford and Worcester. Lions, zebras, giraffes, antelopes, white rhinoceroses, baboons, bears, monkeys, and boat safari.

*Whipsnade Park Zoo*, Dunstable, Bedfordshire. Over 2,000 animals.

*Windsor Safari Park*, St Leonards, Windsor, Berkshire. Lions, giraffes, tigers, elephants, white rhinoceroses and cheetahs.

*Woburn Wild Animal Kingdom*, Woburn Park, Woburn, Bedfordshire. Lions, elephants, antelopes, chimpanzees, bears, elands, tigers, giraffes, white rhinoceroses, monkeys, zebras, hippopotamuses, and wildebeests.

## Scotland

*Loch Lomond Bear Park*, Cameron Estate, Alexandria, Strathclyde. Bears.

*Scotland's African Safari Park*, Stirling Dunblane, Central. Lions, zebras, giraffes, elephants and hippopotamuses.

## Northern Ireland

*Causeway Safari Park*, Dervock, Ballymoney, Antrim. Lions, zebras, elephants, ostriches, pumas and baboons.

Safari park animals seen close up!

# In the Country

## Countryside Commission

The Countryside Commission was set up in 1968 to look after, and improve facilities, for the enjoyment of the countryside in Great Britain. A separate Countryside Commission looks after the conservation and enhancement of selected areas in Scotland.

### National parks

Among the areas for which the Countryside Commission has responsibility are the ten national parks. These are unspoilt regions of outstanding scenery which are conserved for the benefit of the public. Much of the parklands are in fact privately owned, but the Commission advises on how the areas should be improved for the benefit of all. There are at present ten national parks.

**Brecon Beacons** One of the loveliest mountain regions in Britain, situated in the heart of South Wales. It covers an area of 1,344 square kilometres (519 square miles). Most people visit Brecon for its outstanding scenery but the area is also a haven for potholers. It has extensive cave systems, the most famous being that of Dan yr Ogof. There is a mountain centre near Libanus, and information can be obtained from the centres at Abergavenny, Brecon and Llandovery.

**Dartmoor** A region of beautiful and entrancing wildness in the southern part of Devon. It extends over an area of 945 square kilometres (365 square miles). The moors have many items of prehistoric origin but are better known for the rugged outcrops of rock, called *tors*, and the hardy Dartmoor ponies that roam freely throughout the region. During the summer months information about the area can be obtained from vans sited at Ashburton, Haytor, Two Bridges and Yelverton.

**Exmoor** This national park of 686 square kilometres (265 square miles) is in many ways similar to Dartmoor, but is less wild and bleak. The area is often referred to as 'Lorna Doone country' for much of the action in that well-known book takes place on the moor. Information centres are located at Dulverton, Lynmouth and Minehead and there is an information van at Combe Martin.

**Lake District** Covering an area of 2,243 square kilometres (866 square miles) the Lake District is the largest of the national parks. It also, appropriately, boasts the largest lake (Windermere), the highest mountain (Scafell Pike), and the most spectacular mountain scenery in England. Information about the area can be obtained from the National Park centre at Brockhole; information centres at Ambleside,

Bowness and Keswick; and vans at Glenridding, Hawkeshead, and Waterhead.

**Northumberland** The Northumberland National Park consists of 1,031 square kilometres (398 square miles) of rolling moorland and lonely hills. Much of the Pennine Way runs through the Park. The fort on Hadrian's Wall at Housesteads (on B6318 north-west of Haltwhistle on the A69) is a must for anyone interested in Roman history. Information centres are located at Byrness, Ingram, and Once Brewed, and an information van tours the area.

**North Yorkshire Moors** Sheep-cropped moors and rugged, untamed coastline are just two of the features to be admired in the 1,432 square kilometres (553 square miles) of this breathtaking region. One feature that spoils part of the area for many, but which fascinates an equal number of people, is the Fylingdale Early Warning Station on Fylingdale Moor to the west of the A171 which runs along the eastern edge of the Park. The most prominent feature of the station is three large pale globes, which can be seen over a wide area.

**Peak District** The first of the national parks to be established. It comprises 1,404 square kilometres (542 square miles) of untouched hill

*Left:* Snowdon seen from Llyn Padarn, Caernarvonshire.

and dale. The park includes many quiet villages and market towns including the village of Eyam (on the B6521 between the A623 and A625), famous for the brave action of its residents who prevented the Great Plague of 1665–6 from spreading into Derbyshire after it had been brought from London in a trunk of clothes. An information caravan tours the region and there are information centres at Bakewell, Castleton and Edale.

**Pembrokeshire Coast** The smallest and most westerly of all the national parks has 274 kilometres (170 miles) of impressive coastline. In all the park covers an area of 583 square kilometres (225 square miles). The area includes St David's (on the A487) the smallest cathedral city in Britain. There are information centres at Fishguard, Haverfordwest, Kilgetty, Milford Haven, Pembroke, St David's and Tenby.

**Snowdonia** The second largest and most impressive of the national parks consists of 2,188 square kilometres (845 square miles) of awe-inspiring mountain scenery. The most famous of the mountains in the area is Snowdon, which stands 1,085 metres (3,560 feet) high. It is known to the Welsh as Eryri, the place of eagles. There are information centres at Aberdyfi, Bala, Blaenau Ffestiniog, Dolgellau, Harlech, Llanberis and Llanrwst.

**Yorkshire Dales** This national park comprises some 1,760 square kilometres (680 square miles) of undulating moorland and quaint stone villages. Keep a lookout for some of the many fine waterfalls that abound in this region. There are information centres at Aysgarth Falls, Clapham, Malham, and Settle, and there is an information caravan at Hawes.

## Forest parks

There are no national parks in Scotland because the whole of the country has such a wealth of natural beauty it is in effect one enormous national park. Scotland does, however, have five forest parks administered by the Forestry Commission. They are at Glen More in Highland; Argyll, alongside Loch Long; Queen Elizabeth, on the borders of Tayside and Central; Glen Trool, Dumfries and Galloway; and the Border Forest Park which is on the Scotland/England border. There are also forest parks in England and Wales, namely at Snowdonia in North Wales, the Forest of Dean in Gloucestershire, and the New Forest in Hampshire.

Glen Trool forest park.

National Parks and Forest Parks of Great Britain and Ireland.

Areas of outstanding natural beauty

National Parks

△ Irish National Parks

- - - - Long-distance footpaths

Forest Parks

• INVERNESS
Glen More
• ABERDEEN
• FORT WILLIAM
Queen Elizabeth
Argyll
• DUNDEE
• EDINBURGH
• GLASGOW
Northumberland Coast
North Derry
Border Forest
Antrim Coast and Glens
Northumberland
Glen Trool
LONDONDERRY •
CARLISLE
Yorkshire Dales
PENNINE
CLEVELAND WAY
Solway Coast
Sperrin
BELFAST
Lake District
North Yorkshire Moors
South Armagh
Forest of Bowland
WAY
Lecale Coast
Mourne
MANCHESTER •
LEEDS
Phoenix Park △
LIVERPOOL •
GALWAY •
DUBLIN •
Anglesey
Peak District
Norfolk Coast
Snowdonia
OFFA'S DYKE PATH
Cannock Chase
LIMERICK •
Lleyn
• BIRMINGHAM
NORWICH •
Kilkenny Castle Park △ KILKENNY
Cambrian Mountains
Shropshire Hills
Suffolk Coast
Derrynane National Historic Park
Pembrokeshire Coast
Malvern Hills
Dedham Vale
WATERFORD
Brecon Beacons
Dean Forest
Cotswolds
Chilterns
△ △The Bourn Vincent Memorial Park
Wye Valley
LONDON •
NORTH DOWNS WAY
CORK •
Gower
BRISTOL •
△ Garnish Island National Park
PEMBROKESHIRE COAST PATH
Quantock Hills
East Hampshire
Surrey Hills
Kent Downs
• DOVER
North Devon
Sussex Downs
SOUTH DOWNS WAY
Exmoor
Dorset
Bodmin Moor
East Devon
New Forest
Chichester Harbour
Cornwall
• EXETER
Dartmoor
Isle of Wight
SOUTH-WEST PENINSULA COAST PATH

## Other areas of beauty

In addition to the national parks and the forest parks there are a great many areas that are designated as places of outstanding natural beauty. These include much of the coastline of Anglesey in Gwynedd and the outstanding scenery of the Menai Straits that separate the island from the mainland; the pleasant heathlands and woodlands of Cannock Chase in Staffordshire; Chichester Harbour in Sussex and much of the surrounding area from Hayling Island to Apuldram; and 800 square kilometres (309 square miles) of the Chilterns in Oxfordshire and Buckinghamshire. Most of Cornwall is also designated an area of outstanding natural beauty, the reasons for which are self evident to all those who visit the county. Other areas include the Cotswolds, the Gower Peninsula of South Wales, the Isle of Wight, the Kent Downs, the Malvern Hills in Herefordshire and Worcestershire, the coasts of Norfolk and Northumberland, the Quantock Hills in Somerset and the Sussex Downs.

But even this list does not exhaust the many beautiful places to be seen in the British Isles for there are also several national parks in Ireland, some 250 nature reserves, and nearly 2,071 square kilometres (800 square miles) of National Trust properties and gardens. To find out more about the area through which you are travelling consult local guide books, an Ordnance Survey map or a good road atlas, and the local tourist information offices.

Cumbria, one of many areas of beauty.

# The Country Code

### Guard against the risk of fire

Every year a great deal of damage is caused in the countryside by fires that could have been avoided. Do not throw away lit matches or leave bottles. If you build a fire for cooking a meal make sure that it is well and truly extinguished before you leave it.

### Fasten all gates

If you go through a gate make sure that you close it behind you – even if it was open to start with. Farm animals may stray through the open gate and damage crops or wander on to a road and cause a serious accident.

### Keep dogs under control

Animals are easily frightened by dogs, and thousands of sheep are killed each year by dogs that are not properly controlled. A farmer has in certain instances the right by law to shoot a dog that worries his animals.

### Keep to the paths across farmland

If you have to cross a crop field walk around the edge or you will damage the crops.

### Avoid damaging fences, hedges and walls

Apart from the cost to the farmer damaged walls and hedges are equivalent to the open gate – animals can easily stray through the gaps.

### Leave no litter

We live in a beautiful country. Why make it ugly with litter which can also be extremely dangerous to wildlife? Take your litter home with you.

### Safeguard water supplies

Water is important for animals and people. Much of this country's water supply comes from country streams, and polluting the water may put lives at risk.

### Protect all wildlife

Do not pick flowers, disturb wild creatures, or damage trees.

### Go carefully on country roads

The roads may appear deserted, but that is when danger can occur. Another vehicle may appear without warning, people may be walking in the road because there is no footpath, or animals may be on the road.

### Respect the life of the countryside

Have consideration for the inhabitants, both plant and animal, of the countryside. Keep to the Country Code.

# Mills

### Windmills

As you drive through the eastern half of England you will see quite a number of windmills. They were built mainly to turn stone wheels for grinding corn, although some were used to power pumps for draining marshy land. Unfortunately most of them are now in ruins, since their place has been taken by electricity and other more efficient forms of power. In recent years, however, people have come to realise the beauty and historical importance of windmills, and a great deal has been done by various bodies to ensure that many of our windmills are restored to their former glory. There are many individual mills to be seen but all fall into one of three types: post-mill, smock-mill or tower-mill.

The **post-mill**, the earliest type of English windmill first built some 800 years ago, is so called because it is built around a central wooden post.

It was the miller's daily duty to move the building around on its post to catch the wind. If he allowed the wind to hit the mill from behind it could get blown over, a situation known as 'tail-winded'. The first mill of this type was said to have been built in Suffolk in 1191, but the oldest surviving example, built in the fifteenth century, can be seen at Bourn in Cambridgeshire. This mill is open to the public, as is another old post-mill, dated 1627, at Pitstone Green in Buckinghamshire, and there are many other mills of this type to be seen around the country.

The easiest way to recognise a post-mill is by the four brick piers that support four oak beams running up to the central post. Some, however, are not exposed to the elements, the piers being encased in

*Above:* North Leverton tower-mill, Nottinghamshire. *Right:* Nutley post-mill, Sussex. *Far right:* Terling smock-mill, Essex.

a 'roundhouse' which protects the beams and provides storage space.

The **smock-mill** came after the post-mill, and was so called because it was said to look like the billowing smocks worn by farmers in the eighteenth century. In mills of this type only the top portion revolved in the wind. To recognise a smock-mill look for a base made of brick or stone and the upper portion made of wood. You will find that in the majority of cases the smock-mill is octagonal in shape. At the back of

the uppermost portion is a small fantail. The purpose of this fantail is to turn the windmill into the wind – the job that was done by the miller in the old post-mill. A number of fantails were fitted at a later date than the original construction of the mill.

Possibly the finest, and certainly one of the tallest, smock-mills in the British Isles is the Union mill at Cranbrook in Kent. It was built in 1814 but the oldest smock-mill in Britain, built nearly two hundred years earlier, can be seen at Lacey Green in Buckinghamshire.

A **tower-mill** is very similar to the smock-mill but is built entirely of brick or stone. Developed in the eighteenth century, it is usually circular in shape. As in the smock-mill, only the very top portion of a tower-mill revolves in the wind. Some fine examples of tower-mills can be seen at Pakenham in Suffolk, Cley next the Sea in Norfolk, and at Heckington in Lincolnshire. The mill at Heckington has eight sails and is very impressive.

**Annular windmills** are not so romantic as older mills although they can be just as impressive. Apart from mills used for the draining of fenlands most pumping windmills are annular windmills. These have a large number of metal vanes set close together with a fantail at the rear. The construction of such mills usually consists of metal scaffolding with a crankshaft running down the centre of the structure to transmit the power from the revolving vanes to the pumping mechanism.

Keep a look out for windmills on your journeys or, better still, consult an Ordnance Survey map which will tell you the location of windmills along your route (windmills still in use are shown with sails).

## Watermills

Watermills are the oldest means of putting water to work. They were known to the Greeks almost two thousand years ago but were not introduced into Britain until about the ninth century. The action of the water on the wheel was used to turn grinding wheels and a wide range of industrial machinery. There are three types of watermill: overshot, undershot and breast.

In the **overshot** types of watermill, the most common to be seen in Britain, the water hits the wheel at the top and is turned by gravity. The wheel itself consists of a number of curved vanes, or buckets, which carry the water down. When the bucket reaches the bottom of the wheel it spills out the water into the tail race – the part of the stream or the river that comes after the wheel.

How a windmill mechanism works. Wind turns the sails which, by a system of gears, cause the millstones to rotate and so crush the corn.

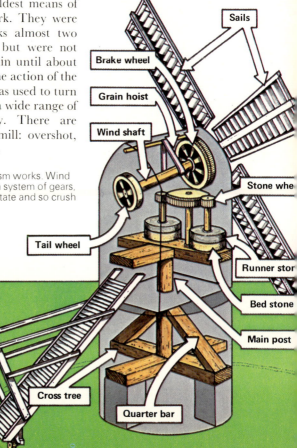

Sails

Brake wheel

Grain hoist

Wind shaft

Stone whe

Fantail or Fly

Tail wheel

Runner stor

Bed stone

Main post

Fan carriage

Cross tree

Quarter bar

Wellbrook mill. The iron-clad breast wheel is 4·9 metres (16 feet) in diameter.

The section of water just before reaching the wheel is called the head race.

An **undershot** watermill needs a fast-flowing water supply to enable it to operate efficiently. With this type the water goes under the wheel and strikes the blades, causing the wheel to revolve. In some wheels the blades are flat, but wheels with curved blades are more efficient.

The **breast** watermill is so called because it has a casing built close to the rim of the wheel between the head race and the tail race. The water enters below the top of the wheel and runs onto vanes, or is caught in buckets. In the vane type the wheel is driven purely by the velocity of the water but where buckets, or curved vanes, are used gravity is the main driving force.

You will find that some waterwheels are built on a man-made channel to the side of the main stream. At the head of the channel is a sluice gate which can be closed to stop the water flow when the mill is not in operation.

# Vehicle Identification

On the pages that follow you will find a valuable pictorial guide to many of the vehicles that can be seen on the road. It has not, of course, been possible to show everything that you are likely to spot on your travels, but it is hoped that it will give you some idea of the wide variety of interesting and intriguing vehicles that can be seen on the roads of the British Isles.

With the specialist vehicles such as tractors, milk floats, and so on, only one or two vehicles of each type have been included. Keep your eyes open when you are travelling on the road and you will be amazed at how much you will see. Things that you never noticed before. Things that will make every journey one of exploration, adventure and excitement.

---

## Motor cars

---

The largest section is naturally devoted to cars because you will see more of these than anything else. Some of the cars included, such as the Lancia Stratos and the Maserati Kyalami, are not at the time of going to press available in this country. It is still possible, however, that you could see them on the road. Such instances will prove extremely rare but the cars have been included to give you something unusual to look out for. On the other hand some of the most popular vehicles have been left out simply because they are so well known. The vehicles that have been included have been selected on the basis that they will provide you with a good cross section of the cars that you are likely to see, and will give you some idea of the variety of different designs that are available.

The fuel consumption and acceleration time quoted should be taken only as a guide to a particular vehicle's performance. These figures rely to a large extent upon the driver's ability, the quality of the particular vehicle, and the conditions prevailing at the time the measurements were made. They may therefore vary slightly from figures quoted in other books and in magazines. Figures marked with an asterisk were not available in this country at the time of going to press.

### Older cars

Many of the cars that you will see on the road will be models that are no longer in production. The majority of the cars you see will, of course, be fairly recent but it is still quite common to see cars that are remarkably old and yet still in good working order. By looking at the registration numbers of these older cars you will be able to determine how old they are (see page 183).

### Veteran and vintage cars

Veteran and vintage cars are usually best seen at rallies and other events that specialise in these 'old faithfuls'. In the majority of cases the owners drive their vehicles to such events and even use them for normal motoring, so it is not unusual to see veteran and vintage vehicles on the roads.

Typical of these is the Austin Seven, which seems to go on forever. This car is now regarded as a collector's item and there is even a special club for Austin Seven owners.

## Electric vehicles

With the price of petrol going ever higher people are beginning to look at alternative forms of power for vehicles. One such form is electricity in the form of batteries. To date, electricity has not proved particu-larly successful with cars because the batteries need recharging after every fifty or so miles. It has, however, proved a useful source of power for town cars, local bus services, and delivery vehicles. And improvement of battery performances in years to come could well result in there being even more electric vehicles on our roads.

Electric vehicles are cheaper to run than petrol- or diesel-powered vehicles. They are also quieter, do not pollute the atmosphere with fumes, are simpler to drive, and suffer fewer breakdowns. Already thousands of electric vehicles are in daily use; you are bound to see some on your travels.

Veteran (built before 1918) and vintage (built from 1918–30) cars.

## Buses and coaches

You cannot travel far without seeing a bus or a coach. Buses, both single and double deckers, operate on what are known as stage or carriage services. In other words they travel along a set route from one fare stage to another and the passengers pay for their journey by obtaining a ticket either from a conductor or, in the case of one-man operated vehicles, the driver. Coaches usually travel greater distances and the ticket is generally paid for in advance. Many of the coaches are run by private companies. Why not see how many different companies you can spot?

Some of the commercial vehicles shown on later pages.

## Lorries

There are a great number of lorries and other goods vehicles on the road, many of them built for specific purposes. Below are some of the different types you will see.

**Tankers** These are specially designed vehicles used for carrying liquids (and some solids). To minimise the potentially dangerous 'wave' effect caused to the moving vehicles by the liquid, large tankers are usually partitioned.

**Artic** Abbreviation for 'articulated vehicle'. The trailer can be detached from the tractor, or cab, unit. Due to the way the trailer is mounted the artic is capable of carrying longer loads than a normal cab with a trailer.

**Juggernaut** General term for a

Motorcycles are now increasingly popular.

large lorry, usually articulated. Many of the juggernauts you will see on the road have come from the Continent. The word 'juggernaut' comes from the Indian god Jagannath whose effigy was dragged through the streets on a mighty cart.

**Rigid** A lorry in which the cab and the goods-carrying part are all one unit. Some bodies completely enclose the load, some have sides that drop down, and some simply consist of a straightforward platform on to which the goods are loaded.

**Refrigerated vehicle** Any of the lorries described above can be refrigerated and used for the transportation of perishable goods. Look for the refrigerating unit mounted at the front of the body.

**Car Transporter** Used to carry cars from the manufacturer to ports and other distribution points. Car transporters can have one or two carrying decks. If you are lucky you may even see one with three carrying decks. Some transporters are rigid,

some are articulated, and some also have trailers.

**Dump Truck** A familiar sight on most building sites, the dump truck is a sturdy vehicle used for carrying earth and rubble. It is recognisable from the headboard that covers the top of the cab to protect the driver. To eject its load the dump truck tips it out by means of a hydraulic device that lifts the front end of the body.

**Luton Van** The type of lorry often used for furniture removals. It is distinguished by the loading space above the driver's cab. The name 'Luton' is said to have been derived from the fact that vans of this type were first used in Luton because the hat manufacturers of the town needed plenty of room in which to pack their straw hats.

## Motorcycles

Motorcycles are becoming increasingly important as a means of personal transport. This upsurge in popularity is in part due to the ever-increasing cost of petrol which is making journeys by motor car particularly expensive when only one person is in the vehicle. It is also due to the fact that motorcycles are now more comfortable than they have been in the past and, of course, they are more manoeuvrable in today's packed traffic conditions. The production figures for 1976 reflected this increase in popularity, for 4,235,112 motorcycles were produced in the world during that year. This represented an 11·4 per cent increase on 1975 figures and it was the second highest production total ever recorded, the highest being 4,509,547 in 1974.

A great variety of vehicles can be seen on the roads.

## Specialised vehicles

A great number of vehicles are made for a very specialised purpose. Among those included in the identification section that follows are ambulances, fire-fighting vehicles and refuse collectors, but there are a great many more to be seen. See how many more you can spot on your travels.

## Fun and leisure vehicles

Motoring should be enjoyable. A short section shows some of the vehicles designed for pleasure and recreation.

**Alfa Romeo Alfasud TI** 4cyl 1186cc
29mpg max 100mph 0–60/14·6sec
length 389cm width 159cm height 137cm
Produced as two-door TI, three-door estate
and four-door saloon.

**Alfa Romeo Alfetta 1·8** 4cyl 1779cc
30mpg max 112mph 0–60/9·5sec
length 428cm width 162cm height 143cm
Also produced in 1·6 version (1570cc max
109mph).

**Alfa Romeo Alfetta GTV 2000** 4cyl
1962cc 25mpg max 120mph 0–60/8·9sec
length 421cm width 166cm height 133cm
Also produced with 1·6 litre engine but this
does not have the ventilation slots on the rear
side

**Alfa Romeo Spider Veloce** 4cyl 1962cc
27mpg max 120mph 0–60/8·9sec
length 412cm width 163cm height 129cm
Also Spider Junior 1300 and 1600 versions.

**American Motors Gremlin** 6cyl 3802cc
21mpg max 100mph 0–60/13·5sec
length 432·6cm width 179cm
height 132·8cm

**American Motors Hornet** 6cyl 3802cc
20mpg max 93mph 0–60/13·7sec
length 455cm width 180cm height 133cm

**American Motors Matador** 6cyl 4229cc
18mpg max 98mph 0–60/15·5sec
length 472cm width 180cm height 133cm

**American Motors Pacer** 6cyl 3802cc
14·7mpg max 90mph 0–60/13·7sec
length 432cm width 196cm height 134cm
Has three doors. The driver's door is wider
than the passenger's.

**Aston Martin Lagonda** V8 cyl 5340cc
13mpg max 150mph 0–60/5·7sec
length 528cm width 182cm height 130·2cm
Called the 'space age car' because of its many
computerised controls.

**Aston Martin V8** V8 cyl 5340cc 14mpg
max 150mph 0–60/6·2sec length 465cm
width 183cm height 133cm

**Audi 100** 4 cyl 1984cc 30mpg
max 110mph 0–60/10·1sec length 468cm
width 176·8cm height 139·3cm Audi 80
similar in style but shorter (420cm) and not so
powerful (max 92mph).

**Austin Allegro 1300** 4 cyl 1275cc 35mpg
max 83mph 0–60/17·4sec length 385cm
width 161cm height 139·5cm Also with 1100,
1500 and 1750cc engines.

**Austin Maxi** 4 cyl 1748cc 28mpg
max 95mph 0–60/15·5sec length 402cm
width 162cm height 138cm Also with 1500cc
engine (max 90mph 0–60, 17sec).

**Bentley T Series** V8 cyl 6750cc 15mpg
max 110mph 0–60/10·5sec length 516·9cm
width 180·3cm height 151·7cm Four-door
models are powered by same engine as the
Rolls-Royce Silver Shadow.

**BMW 528** 6 cyl 2788cc 25mpg
max 122mph 0–60/8sec length 462cm
width 168·9cm height 142·5cm Other
'5-series' models are the 518, 520, 520i (the i
indicates fuel injection) and the 525.

**BMW 3·0Si** 6 cyl 2985cc 23mpg
max 132mph 0–60/7·4sec length 470cm
width 175·3cm height 144·8cm One of the
fastest production four-door saloons in the
world.

**BMW 633** 6 cyl 3210cc 22mpg
max 130mph 0–60/7·8sec length 475·5cm
width 172·5cm height 136·5cm 'Check' lights
on the dashboard tell the driver how well vital
parts of the engine are functioning.

**Bristol 412** V8 cyl 6556cc 15mpg
max 140mph 0–60/7·5sec length 490cm
width 177cm height 144cm Convertible
styled by the Italian coachbuilder Zagato.

**Buick Riviera** V8 cyl 6604cc 14mpg
max 105mph 0–60/9·8sec length 554·4cm
width 192cm height 138·4cm

**Cadillac Seville** V8 cyl 5700cc 12mpg
max 112mph 0–60/12·2sec length 518·2cm
width 182·4cm height 138·9cm
'European-sized' Cadillac first introduced in
1975.

**Chevrolet Monza** 4 cyl 2294cc 12·5mpg
max *mph 0–60/10·4sec length 460cm
width 168cm height 129cm

**Chevrolet Camaro** 6 cyl 4096cc 17mpg
max 100mph 0–60/14·2sec length 497·5cm
width 189·7cm height 125cm

**Chevrolet Impala** 6 cyl 4096cc 18·5mpg
max 90mph 0–60/15·3sec length 538·5cm
width 193cm height 142cm

**Chevrolet Monza Spyder** V8 cyl 5000cc
12·5mpg max *mph 0–60/10·4sec
length 455·5cm width 166cm
height 127·5cm

### Chevrolet Corvette
V8 cyl 5735cc 15mpg max 120mph 0–60/8·9sec length 470·5cm width 175cm height 122cm

### Chevrolet Caprice
V8 cyl 5736cc 15mpg max 116mph 0–60/11·5sec length 539cm width 192cm height 145·4cm

### Chrysler Avenger
4 cyl 1295cc 31mpg max 85mph 0–60/17sec length 409cm width 158·8cm height 140·8cm Restyled in 1977 with new front end, rear lights and instrument display.

### Chrysler Alpine
4 cyl 1294cc 38mpg max 95mph 0–60/15·6sec length 424·5cm width 168cm height 140cm Produced both in England and France, this car has won several design awards. Also with 1442cc engine.

### Chrysler 2 litre
4 cyl 1981cc 25mpg max 100mph 0–60/14sec length 452cm width 172·7cm height 142·2cm Designed in Coventry, made in Spain.

### Citroen 2 CV
Flat twin cyl 602cc 50mpg max 70mph 0–60/30·5sec length 380cm width 148cm height 160cm First produced in 1948 and still a popular car.

### Citroen Dyane
2 cyl 602cc 48mpg max 72mph 0–60/29·2sec length 390cm width 150cm height 154cm Introduced in 1967. Has a roll-back rag top.

### Citroen GS Pallas
4 cyl 1222cc 30mpg max 90mph 0–60/16sec length 412cm width 161cm height 135cm Also with 1015cc engine.

**Citroen CX 2400** 4 cyl 2347cc 20mpg
max 110mph 0–60/15·5sec length 460cm
width 173cm height 136cm Also in saloon
and estate, petrol or diesel versions.

**Colt Lancer** 4 cyl 1238cc 33mpg
max 93mph 0–60/14·5sec length 398cm
width 152·5cm height 136cm Also produced
with 1439cc and 1597cc engines.

**Colt Celeste** 4 cyl 1597cc 35mpg
max 100mph 0–60/11·5sec length 411·5cm
width 160·7cm height 132·8cm Made by
Mitsubishi of Japan. Also with 1995cc engine
and five-speed gearbox.

**Colt Sigma** 4 cyl 1597cc 30mpg
max 98mph 0–60/14·5sec length 429cm
width 165·7cm height 136cm Introduced
1976. Also with 1995cc engine.

**Daimler Sovereign** 6 cyl 4235cc 16mpg
max 120mph 0–60/10·5sec length 484·3cm
width 177cm height 137·5cm

**Daimler Double Six** V12 cyl 5343cc
15mpg max 140mph 0–60/7·5sec
length 494·5cm width 177cm height 137·5cm
Based on Jaguar XJ 5·3, the Double Six is one
of the fastest production cars in the world.

**Datsun 100A Cherry** 4 cyl 988cc 40mpg
max 85mph 0–60/16·5sec length 365·8cm
width 149·8cm height 137·2cm Two-door
saloon, 4-door saloon and estate.

**Datsun Cherry F-11 Coupe** 4 cyl 1171cc
30mpg max 93mph 0–60/9sec
length 382cm width 150·5cm
height 130·8cm Introduced 1976 with same
transverse engine and front drive unit as
Datsun 120A.

**Datsun 120Y Sunny** 4cyl 1171cc 30mpg
max 93mph 0–60/17sec length 395cm
width 155cm height 137·2cm

**Datsun 140J Violet** 4cyl 1428cc 34mpg
max 94mph 0–60/15sec length 411·5cm
width 157·5cm height 139·7cm

**Datsun 260Z** 6cyl 2565cc 23mpg
max 125mph 0–60/8·8sec length 442cm
width 163cm height 128·5cm

**Datsun Laurel** 6cyl 1998cc 30mpg
max 100mph 0–60/14·8sec length 450cm
width 166·8cm height 141cm

**De Tomaso Pantera GTS** V8cyl 5763cc
15mpg max 170mph 0–60/5·6sec
length 426·7cm width 183cm height 109cm
Introduced 1970.

**Dodge Aspen** 6cyl 3688cc *mpg
max *mph 0–60/*sec length 501·6cm
width 185cm height 135cm Produced as
two-door coupe, four-door sedan and
four-door station wagon.

**Dodge Coronet** 6cyl 3688cc 20mpg
max 95mph 0–60/14·5sec length 557cm
width 198cm height 137·7cm Produced as
four door sedan or station wagon, also with
5212cc, 5900cc, and 6556cc engines.

**Dodge Dart** 6cyl 3688cc 20mpg
max 98mph 0–60/14·3sec length 516·6cm
width 177cm height 137cm

**Ferrari 308 GTB** V8 cyl 2926cc 20mpg
max 155mph 0–60/6·4sec length 423cm
width 172cm height 112cm Developed from
and mechanically similar to the Dino 308, but
with body styled by Pininfarina.

**Ferrari 365 GT4** V12 cyl 4390cc 11mpg
max 155mph 0–60/5·4sec length 480cm
width 179cm height 129cm

**Fiat 126** 2 cyl 594cc 50mpg max 63mph
0–60/40sec length 305·4cm width 137·8cm
height 130cm Introduced 1972, almost 60% of
Fiat's compact and economical models are
driven by women.

**Fiat 127** 4 cyl 903cc 40mpg max 85mph
0–60/17·2sec length 359·4cm
width 152·4cm height 137cm Ford engineers
working on the Fiesta were strongly
influenced by this lively little car.

**Fiat 128** 4 cyl 1290cc 30mpg max 95mph
0–60/11·3sec length 385·4cm
width 158·7cm height 142·2cm Introduced
1970. Available in saloon, estate, and coupe
styles, also with 1116cc engine.

**Fiat 131 Mirafiori** 4 cyl 1585cc 32mpg
max 95mph 0–60/13·3sec length 426·7cm
width 165·1cm height 139·7cm Introduced
1974. Also with 1297cc engine (0–60, 14·7sec
max 91mph).

**Fiat 132** 4 cyl 1755cc 28mpg max 100mph
0–60/11·5sec length 439·4cm
width 163·8cm height 144cm

**Fiat X1/9** 4 cyl 1290cc 26mpg
max 105mph 0–60/11·8sec length 383cm
width 157·5cm height 117cm

**Ford Fiesta** 4 cyl 957cc 40mpg
max 80mph 0–60/16·1sec length 356·5cm
width 156·7cm height 131·4cm Built in
Britain, Spain and Germany.

**Ford Escort** 4 cyl 1298cc 35mpg
max 88mph 0–60/15·8sec length 397·8cm
width 139·5cm height 136·6cm Available in
several versions and engine sizes.

**Ford Cortina Saloon** 4 cyl 1593cc 30mpg
max 95mph 0–60/14sec length 433cm
width 170cm height 136cm Available in
several versions and engine sizes.

**Ford Capri** 4 cyl 1593cc 30mpg
max 95mph 0–60/14·5sec length 427·5cm
width 170cm height 130cm Available in
several versions and engine sizes.

**Ford Granada** 4 cyl 1993cc 30mpg
max 95mph 0–60/17sec length 467·4cm
width 179cm height 139·7cm Available in a
variety of versions and engine sizes.

**Hillman Hunter** 4 cyl 1725cc 35mpg
max 90mph 0–60/15·5sec length 439·4cm
width 161·3cm height 142·2cm

**Honda Civic** 4 cyl 1169cc 40mpg
max 85mph 0–60/16sec length 356cm
width 150·5cm height 132·5cm Introduced
1972. Four-door 1488cc version (42mpg
max 90mph 0–60, 13sec) introduced two
years later.

**Honda Accord** 4 cyl 1599cc 30mpg
max 95mph 0–60/12sec length 412·5cm
width 162cm height 134cm

**Jaguar 3·4** 6 cyl 3442cc 20mpg
max 117mph 0–60/13·2sec length 494·5cm
width 177·5cm height 137·5cm The smallest
engined Jaguar.

**Jaguar XJ12** V12 cyl 5343cc 15mpg
max 144mph 0–60/8sec length 484·3cm
width 177cm height 137·5cm

**Jaguar XJ-S** V12 cyl 5343cc 18mpg
max 150mph 0–60/6·8sec length 487cm
width 179cm height 126cm

**Lada** 4 cyl 1198cc 30mpg max 85mph
0–60/16·8sec length 407cm width 162·6cm
height 140cm Made in Russia; inspired by and
almost identical in appearance to Italian Fiat
124. Also with 1452cc engine.

**Lamborghini Urraco** V8 cyl 2996cc
15mpg max 165mph 0–60/6·2sec
length 428·5cm width 174cm height 116cm

**Lamborghini Silhouette** V8 cyl 2998cc
16mpg max 150mph 0–60/6·5sec
length 426·7cm width 182·9cm
height 111·7cm

**Lamborghini Espada** V12 cyl 3929cc
18mpg max 155mph 0–60/7sec
length 474cm width 186cm height 118cm

**Lamborghini Countach LP 400** V12 cyl
3929cc 14mpg max 185mph 0–60/5·4sec
length 417cm width 188·5cm
height 109·5cm Introduced 1971.

**Lancia Beta** 4 cyl 1297cc 26mpg
max 100mph 0–60/14sec length 429·5cm
width 169cm height 140cm

**Lancia Beta Coupe** 4 cyl 1592cc 28mpg
max 115mph 0–60/11sec length 400cm
width 165cm height 128cm

**Lancia Monte Carlo** 4 cyl 1995cc 29mpg
max 120mph 0–60/9sec length 381cm
width 170cm height 118·4cm

**Lancia Stratos** V6 cyl 2418cc *mpg
max 145mph 0–60/*sec length 371cm
width 175cm height 111cm

**Lancia Gamma** 4 cyl 2484cc 28·6mpg
max 122mph 0–60/9·8sec length 458cm
width 173cm height 141cm Four-door saloon
and two-door coupe styled by Pininfarina.

**Land Rover Estate Wagon** 4 cyl 2286cc
16mpg max 66mph 0–60/27·5sec
length 362cm width 168cm height 194cm

**Lotus Eclat** 4 cyl 1973cc 28mpg
max 130mph 0–60/8sec length 446cm
width 181·6cm height 120cm

**Lotus Elite** 4 cyl 1973cc 26mpg
max 125mph 0–60/7·9sec length 446cm
width 182cm height 121cm Identical engine
used for Lotus Eclat.

**Lotus Esprit** 4 cyl 1973cc 33mpg
max 138mph 0–60/6·8sec length 422cm
width 183cm height 109·5cm Glass fibre
body designed by Giugiaro.

**Maserati Merak** V6 cyl 2965cc 13mpg
max 150mph 0–60/7·5sec length 433cm
width 177cm height 113cm First introduced
in 1972.

**Maserati Kyalami** V8 cyl 4136cc 20mpg
max 150mph 0–60/*sec length 358cm
width 185cm height 124·5cm

**Maserati Bora** V8 cyl 4930cc 14mpg
max 160mph 0–60/6·5sec length 433cm
width 173·5cm height 115·5cm

**Mazda 1000** 4 cyl 985cc 36mpg
max 76mph 0–60/20sec length 385·5cm
width 154cm height 138·5cm Also produced
with 1272cc engine as four-door saloon and
five-door estate.

**Mazda 818** 4 cyl 1272cc 32mpg
max 95mph 0–60/15sec length 407·5cm
width 159·5cm height 138cm Two-door
coupe, four-door saloon and five-door estate
all with identical front ends.

**Mazda 616** 4 cyl 1586cc 32mpg
max 100mph 0–60/13·5sec length 426cm
width 158cm height 143·5cm

**Mazda 929** 4 cyl 1769cc 28mpg
max 95mph 0–60/13·5sec length 440·5cm
width 166·5cm height 138cm Two-door
coupe, four-door saloon and five-door estate.

**Mercedes-Benz 280 E** 6 cyl 2746cc
23mpg max 124mph 0–60/9·5sec
length 472·5cm width 178cm
height 143·8cm

**Mercedes-Benz 350 SL** V8 cyl 3499cc
22mpg max 125mph 0–60/8·2sec
length 437cm width 179cm height 130cm
Same bodywork as 450 SL but with smaller
engine.

**Mercedes-Benz 450 SEL** V8 cyl 4520cc
15mpg max 135mph 0–60/9sec
length 506cm width 186cm height 142cm
Awarded 'Car of the Year' in 1973.

**MG Midget** 4 cyl 1493cc 30mpg
max 100mph 0–60/13·9sec length 358cm
width 139cm height 123cm First introduced
1961.

**MGB** 4 cyl 1798cc 26mpg max 105mph
0–60/12sec length 402cm width 152cm
height 129·5cm Open two-seater model first
introduced 1962. Coupe version has folding
rear seats.

**MGB GT V8** V8 cyl 3528cc 20mpg
max 125mph 0–60/7·7sec length 402cm
width 151·3cm height 129·5cm

**Mini** 4 cyl 848cc 37mpg max 70mph
0–60/25sec length 305cm width 140cm
height 135cm Range includes 998cc, 1098cc
(Clubman) and 1275cc (GT) engines.
Designed by Alec Issigonis.

**Morgan 4–4** 4 cyl 1599cc 26mpg
max 100mph 0–60/10·5sec length 360cm
width 142cm height 129cm Open two-seater
tourer. Also produced in a four-seater version.

**Morgan Plus 8** V8 cyl 3528cc 24mpg max 125mph 0–60/6·8sec length 373·4cm width 157·5cm height 132cm Bodywork is coach-built on a wooden frame. Engine is same as used in the Rover 3500.

**Morris Marina** 4 cyl 1275cc 35mpg max 85mph 0–60/17·5sec length 422cm width 164cm height 142cm Several versions produced.

**Moskvich 412** 4cyl 1478cc 26mpg max 92mph 0–60/15·3sec length 420cm width 155·6cm height 148cm

**NSU RO 80** 1990 cc 18mpg max 112mph 0–60, 12·4sec length 478cm width 176cm height 141cm Powered by Wankel rotary engine.

**Opel Kadett J City** 4 cyl 1196cc 33mpg max 82mph 0–60/17·8sec length 389·2cm width 157cm height 138cm

**Opel Manta** 4 cyl 1897cc 28mpg max 104mph 0–60/11sec length 444·5cm width 167cm height 133cm

**Opel Ascona Berlina** 4 cyl 1897cc 30mpg max 104mph 0–60/11sec length 432cm width 167cm height 138cm Introduced 1976.

**Opel Commodore** 6 cyl 2784cc 20mpg max 115mph 0–60/10sec length 460·5cm width 172·7cm height 140·5cm Six cylinder version of the Opel Rekord.

**Panther Lima** 4cyl 2279cc 28mpg
max 110mph 0–60/7·5sec length 360·7cm
width 162cm height 122cm Introduced 1976.
Uses same engine as Vauxhall Magnum 2300.

**Panther J72** 6cyl 4235cc 20mpg
max 130mph 0–60/6·5sec length 409cm
width 196cm height 124cm

**Panther De Ville** V12cyl 4235cc 15mpg
max 130mph 0–60/12·5sec length 518cm
width 180·3cm height 154·9cm Also
produced as a four-door saloon.

**Peugeot 104** 4cyl 1124cc 30mpg
max 96mph 0–60/17sec length 336cm
width 152cm height 140cm

**Peugeot 304** 4cyl 1290cc 25mpg
max 93mph 0–60/14sec length 399cm
width 157·5cm height 143·5cm Introduced
1969.

**Peugeot 504** 4cyl 1796cc 30mpg
max 97mph 0–60/16sec length 448cm
width 169cm height 146cm Also available
1971cc and 1948cc diesel engine.

**Peugeot 604** V6cyl 2664cc 23mpg
max 113mph 0–60/12·5sec length 472cm
width 177cm height 143cm

**Polski Fiat** 4cyl 1481cc 30mpg
max 90mph 0–60/15sec length 422·6cm
width 163cm height 144cm Similar to Fiat
125. Made in Poland.

**Pontiac Firebird Trans-Am** V8 cyl
6556cc 12mpg max 120mph 0–60/8·4sec
length 498cm width 185·4cm height 128cm

**Porsche 911** 6cyl 2687cc 20mpg
max 130mph 0–60/7sec length 428cm
width 161cm height 132cm Introduced 1964.

**Porsche 924** 4cyl 1984cc 28mpg
max 125mph 0–60/8·5sec length 420cm
width 155·6cm height 127cm

**Porsche Carrera** 6cyl 2993cc 22mpg
max 145mph 0–60/6sec length 429·1cm
width 165·2cm height 132cm

**Porsche Turbo** 6cyl 2993cc 19mpg
max 155mph 0–60/5sec length 429cm
width 177·5cm height 132cm

**Princess 1800** 4cyl 1798cc 26mpg
max 97mph 0–60/15sec length 445·5cm
width 173cm height 141cm Similar in
appearance to Princess 2200 but with round
headlights.

**Princess 2200** 6cyl 2227cc 25mpg
max 105mph 0–60/13sec length 445·5cm
width 173cm height 141cm

**Reliant Robin** 4cyl 850cc 45mpg
max 72mph 0–60/24·5sec length 333cm
width 137cm height 142cm Three wheeled
car. First introduced 1973.

**Reliant Kitten** 4 cyl 848cc 50mpg
max 80mph 0–60/18·5sec length 333cm
width 142cm height 140cm Same engine as
in Reliant Robin.

**Reliant Scimitar** V6 cyl 2994cc 28mpg
max 120mph 0–60/9sec length 443·2cm
width 170·8cm height 132cm

**Renault 4** 4 cyl 845cc 37mpg max 70mph
0–60/25sec length 369cm width 148·6cm
height 154·9cm Produced in two versions, 4L
and 4TL.

**Renault 5 GTL** 4 cyl 1289cc 50mpg
max 90mph 0–60/15·5sec length 350cm
width 152cm height 140cm Also produced as
5L (845cc), 5TL (956cc) and 5TS (1289cc).

**Renault 12** 4 cyl 1289cc 25mpg
max 90mph 0–60/14sec length 434cm
width 161cm height 143cm

**Renault 14** 4 cyl 1218cc 35mpg
max 88mph 0–60/15sec length 401·5cm
width 160cm height 137cm

**Renault 15** 4 cyl 1289cc 30mpg
max 93mph 0–60/13·5sec length 426cm
width 163cm height 131cm Similar to
Renault 17.

**Renault 16 TX** 4 cyl 1647cc 35mpg
max 104mph 0–60/12sec length 423·5cm
width 162·5cm height 145cm Introduced in
1965. Available in several versions.

**Renault 20 TL** 4 cyl 1647cc 30mpg
max 100mph 0–60/17sec length 452cm
width 173·2cm height 143·5cm

**Renault 30 TS** V6 cyl 2664cc 20mpg
max 110mph 0–60/9·7sec length 452cm
width 172·7cm height 142·2cm

**Rolls Royce Silver Shadow** V8 cyl
6750cc 15mpg max 120mph 0–60/10·5sec
length 517cm width 180cm height 152cm

**Rolls Royce Corniche** V8 cyl 6750cc
14mpg max 120mph 0–60/9·5sec
length 517cm width 183cm height 148·6cm
Similar to Bentley Corniche.

**Rolls Royce Camargue** V8 cyl 6750cc
14mpg max 120mph 0–60/9·5sec
length 517cm width 192cm height 147cm

**Rover 2000** 4 cyl 1978cc 25mpg
max 98mph 0–60/14·5sec length 479cm
width 171cm height 140cm

**Rover 3500** V8 cyl 3528cc 24mpg
max 120mph 0–60/9·5sec length 470cm
width 177cm height 135cm

**Range Rover** V8 cyl 3528cc 20mpg
max 99mph 0–60/15sec length 447cm
width 178cm height 178cm

**Saab 96 L**  V4 cyl  1498cc  30mpg
max 90mph  0–60/17·5sec  length 430cm
width 159cm  height 147cm  First introduced
1966.

**Saab 99**  4 cyl  1985cc  30mpg  max 102mph
0–60/12·8sec  length 442cm  width 169cm
height 144cm  Anti-theft device locks the
gearbox.

**Saab EMS**  4 cyl  1985cc  30mpg
max 110mph  0–60/10sec  length 442cm
width 169cm  height 143·5cm

**Simca 1000**  4 cyl  994cc  35mpg
max 80mph  0–60/21sec  length 381·4cm
width 148·5cm  height 136·5cm  Also
produced with 1118cc and 1294cc engines.

**Simca 1100**  4 cyl  1118cc  34mpg
max 87mph  0–60/14sec  length 394cm
width 158cm  height 146cm

**Skoda S110R**  4 cyl  1107cc  36mpg
max 90mph  0–60/18·5sec  length 415·5cm
width 162cm  height 134·1cm  Made in
Czechoslovakia.

**Toyota 1000**  4 cyl  993cc  35mpg
max 87mph  0–60/17·5sec  length 369cm
width 145cm  height 138cm

**Toyota Corolla Liftback**  4 cyl  1166cc
35mpg  max 90mph  0–60/18·5sec
length 408cm  width 161·5cm  height 132cm
The best selling car in the world in 1975.

**Toyota Carina** 4 cyl 1588cc 30mpg
max 100mph 0–60/12·2sec length 420·5cm
width 159·5cm height 138·5cm

**Toyota Celica** 4 cyl 1588cc 36mpg
max 100mph 0–60/13·5sec length 426cm
width 162cm height 131cm

**Toyota 2000** 4 cyl 1968cc 30mpg
max 100mph 0–60/15sec length 424·5cm
width 161cm height 140cm

**Toyota Crown Estate** 6 cyl 2563cc
20mpg max 100mph 0–60/12·5sec
length 469cm width 169cm height 150cm
Also produced as a saloon with similar
specifications.

**Triumph Dolomite** 4 cyl 1296cc 36mpg
max 85mph 0–60/18·5sec length 412·7cm
width 166·4cm height 137·2cm Originally
known as the Triumph Toledo. Produced in
three versions, 1300, 1500 and 1500 HL.

**Triumph Dolomite Sprint** 4 cyl 1998cc
26mpg max 112mph 0–60/9·2sec
length 411·5cm width 158·7cm
height 137·2cm Similar is the 1850 HL
Dolomite (1854cc 30mpg max 100mph
0–60, 11·5sec).

**Triumph Spitfire** 4 cyl 1493cc 33mpg
max 100mph 0–60/13sec length 378cm
width 148·8cm height 116·2cm Introduced
1962, 1500 model launched in 1974.

**Triumph Stag** V8 cyl 2997cc 26mpg
max 110mph 0–60/10sec length 441·3cm
width 161·3cm height 125·7cm Detachable
hard-top or soft-top versions.

**Triumph TR7** 4 cyl 1998cc 29mpg max 110mph 0–60/9·4sec length 417·3cm width 168·1cm height 126·7cm Has same gearbox as Rover 3500.

**TVR 3000 M** V6 cyl 2994cc 30mpg max 126mph 0–60/7·5sec length 417cm width 162·6cm height 119·4cm Handmade sports car. First introduced 1972.

**Vanden Plas 1500** 4 cyl 1485cc 25mpg max 85mph 0–60/16·4sec length 392cm width 161cm height 139cm Based on the Allegro 1500 but distinguished by its radiator grille.

**Vauxhall Chevette** 4 cyl 1256cc 32mpg max 90mph 0–60/15·5sec length 417·8cm width 157cm height 131cm Variations of the same design built in Japan, U.S.A., Germany and South America.

**Vauxhall Viva** 4 cyl 1256cc 35mpg max 85mph 0–60/18·5sec length 413·8cm width 164·3cm height 135cm Same engine as in Vauxhall Chevette.

**Vauxhall Magnum** 4 cyl 1759cc 28mpg max 95mph 0–60/15sec length 415·3cm width 164·3cm height 133·6cm Similar to Viva but with four headlights, styled wheels and a more powerful engine.

**Vauxhall VX 2300** 4 cyl 2279cc 25mpg max 100mph 0–60/12sec length 457·2cm width 169·9cm height 135·4cm Successor to the Victor which ceased production in 1975.

**Volkswagen Polo** 4 cyl 895cc 37mpg max 83mph 0–60/18sec length 350·5cm width 156·2cm height 133·4cm

**Volkswagen 1200** 4 cyl 1192cc 41 mpg
max 71·6mph 0–50/16·9sec length 408cm
width 155cm height 150cm

**Volkswagen Golf** 4 cyl 1096cc 28mpg
max 84mph 0–60/17·8sec length 373
cm width 161cm height 141cm Produced in
several versions and engine sizes.

**Volkswagen Passat** 4 cyl 1588cc 30mpg
max 100mph 0–60/16sec length 422cm
width 160cm height 136cm

**Volkswagen Scirocco** 4 cyl 1588cc
30mpg max 110mph 0–60/10·8sec
length 388·5cm width 162·5cm
height 131cm

**Volvo 66 GL** 4 cyl 1289cc 38mpg
max 85mph 0–60/19·5sec length 266cm
width 154cm height 138cm Volvo's smallest
car, originally the Daf 66.

**Volvo 343** 4 cyl 1397cc 35mpg
max 90mph 0–60/14·3sec length 420cm
width 166cm height 144cm

**Volvo 244** 4 cyl 2127cc 26mpg
max 100mph 0–60/14·5sec length 490cm
width 170·7cm height 145·5cm Introduced
1974.

**Volvo 264** V6 cyl 2664cc 20mpg
max 100mph 0–60/15·5sec length 490cm
width 170·2cm height 143·5cm Introduced
1974. Also produced as a five-door estate, the
265.

**Alfa Romeo GT1300 Junior** 4 cyl 1290cc
28·8mpg max 109mph 0–60/11sec
length 408cm width 158cm height 131·5cm
Also with 1570cc engine.

**American Motors Javelin** 6 cyl 3802cc
20·9mpg max 99mph 0–60/*sec
length 485cm width 182·6cm
height 130·9cm Several versions produced.

**Austin A30** 4 cyl 850cc 35mpg
max 68mph 0–60/30sec Produced 1951.

**Austin A40** 4 cyl 948cc 36·5mpg
max 75·2mph 0–60/29sec length 369·6cm
width 149·9cm height 154·5cm Produced in
1958.

**Austin A60** 4 cyl 1622cc 25·1mpg
max 80·4mph 0–60/19·8sec length 443·2cm
width 160cm height 148·6cm Popular deluxe
saloon.

**Austin 1100** 4 cyl 1098cc 34mpg
max 78·2mph 0–60/23·5sec length 372·1cm
width 152·4cm height 135·6cm Many similar
models produced.

**Austin Metropolitan** 4 cyl 950cc 40mpg
max 75mph 0–60/23sec length 380cm
width 150·5cm height 142cm Combination of
British and American styling.

**Austin Healey Sprite** 4 cyl 948cc 38mpg
max 85mph 0–60/18·5sec Mark 1 produced
in 1958.

**Citroen D19 Special** 4 cyl 1985cc
23·3mpg max 94mph 0–60/15sec
length 487cm width 180cm height 147cm
Luxury French car

**Citroen Light 15** 4 cyl 1900cc *mpg
max *mph 0–60/*sec length *cm width *cm
height *cm Pre-war car with front-wheel drive.

**Ford Anglia Super** 4 cyl 1198cc 33mpg
max 80mph 0–60/21·6sec length 391·2cm
width 144·8cm height 142·2cm Also
available as an estate car.

**Ford Consul Mk II** 4 cyl 1703cc 23mpg
max 73mph 0–60/29·5sec length 443·9cm
width 174·6cm height 153cm Also made as
convertible and estate car.

**Ford Corsair** 4 cyl 1498cc 30mpg
max 83mph 0–60/19sec length 458·5cm
width 161·9cm height 144·1cm
Medium-sized luxury model.

**Ford Mustang** 6 cyl 3277cc 19·9mpg
max 96mph 0–60/13sec length 476cm
width 182·1cm height 128·5cm Many
versions of this American Ford available.

**Ford Popular** 4 cyl 1172cc 31·5mpg
max 72mph 0–60/36·1sec length 381·6cm
width 154·3cm height 149·2cm World's
cheapest four-seater family car when
produced.

**Fiat 500** 2 cyl 499cc 53·4mpg max 63mph
0–60/*sec length 297cm width 132cm
height 132·5cm Popular all over Europe.

### Hillman Imp
4 cyl 875cc 43·7mpg max 80mph 0–60/22·9sec length 353cm width 153cm height 138·4cm Rear-engined answer to the mini.

### Humber Super Snipe
6 cyl 2965cc 15·8mpg max 97·8mph 0–60/16·2sec length 478·8cm width 176·5cm height 155·2cm Large luxury saloon showing American influence in its design.

### Jaguar XK120
6 cyl 3442cc 20mpg max 125mph 0–60/*sec length 440cm width 156cm height *cm Classic post-war sports car.

### Jaguar Mk II
6 cyl 2483cc 17·1mpg max 105·8mph 0–60/11·7sec length 455·9cm width 168·9cm height 146cm Also produced in larger engine sizes.

### Jaguar E-type
6 cyl 3781cc 19·7mpg max 150·1mph 0–60/7·1sec length 446·2cm width 165·7cm height 119·4cm Developed from racing Jaguars.

### Lancia Fulvia Coupe 1·6HF
4 cyl 1100cc 28·5mpg max 115mph 0–60/*sec length 395·5cm width 157cm height 133cm Stylish coupe also successfully rallied.

### Lotus Elan S4
4 cyl 1558cc 15·4mpg max 120mph 0–60/7·3sec length 368·3cm width 142·2cm height 114·9cm Fast fibre-glass bodied car with Lotus developed Ford engine.

### Mercedes 230SL
6 cyl 2306cc 18·5mpg max 115·3mph 0–60/11·5sec length 431·2cm width 175·3cm height 132·1cm Sports coupé with uniquely styled roof.

**Messerschmitt Tg 500** This four wheeled 'bubble car', produced from 1958 to 1960, has a 500cc twin-cylinder engine.

**MGA** 1600cc max 100mph This two seater roadster, first produced in 1956, was the forerunner to the popular MGB which made its first appearance in 1963.

**MG TF Midget** Two seater roadster introduced in 1954. Its four cylinder engine had a displacement of 1250cc and a maximum speed of 80mph.

**Morris Minor** 4 cyl 1098cc 37mpg max 80mph 0–50/15sec length 376cm width 155cm height 152cm

**Riley Elf Mk2** 4 cyl 998cc 36mpg max 76mph 0–50/15.2sec length 325cm width 140cm height 133cm

**Rover 80** 4 cyl 2286cc 19mpg max 83mph 0–50/15.1sec length 445cm width 163cm height 155cm

**Singer Vogue** 4 cyl 1725cc 34mpg max 90mph 0–50/9.9sec length 430cm width 161cm height 142cm

**Standard Vanguard** 4 cyl 2100cc In production from 1947 to 1961. It was replaced in 1960 by the Vanguard Six which had a similar appearance.

### Sunbeam Rapier 4 cyl 1725cc 31 mpg
max 103mph 0–50/9sec length 443cm width 165cm height 140cm

### Triumph Herald 1200 4 cyl 1147cc
40mpg max 80mph 0–50/15·5sec length 389cm width 153cm height 140cm

### Triumph Roadster The body of this two
seater roadster of 1954 was styled by W. J. Belgrove. With a four cylinder engine of 1991cc it could achieve 105mph.

### Triumph TR5 6 cyl 2500cc Introduced in
1968, the TR5 engine replaced the 2·1 litre Standard Vanguard engine previously used in the TR range.

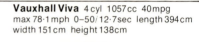

### Triumph 2000 6 cyl 1998cc 24mpg
max 100mph 0–50/9·8sec length 463cm width 165cm height 142cm

### Vauxhall Viva 4 cyl 1057cc 40mpg
max 78·1mph 0–50/12·7sec length 394cm width 151cm height 138cm

### Volkswagen Beetle 4 cyl 1285cc 35mpg
max 75mph 0–60/25·5sec length 403cm width 155cm height 150cm

### Volvo P1800S 4 cyl 1780cc 24mpg
max 106mph 0–50/10·1sec length 430cm width 165cm height 125cm

**Alvis 12/50** This model was first introduced in 1924. Its four cylinder engine had a displacement of 1645cc and its maximum speed was 78mph.

**Austin 7** The first Seven, designed by Herbert Austin himself, was produced in 1922. Its four cylinder, 698cc engine produced a maximum speed of 45–50mph.

**Bentley 4½** This 4½ litre supercharged car was introduced in 1928. 4 cyl 4398cc length 488cm width 175cm max speed 90mph (later increased to 130mph).

**Hispano Suiza Alfonso** Named after King Alfonso XIII of Spain. First models built in Barcelona in 1912. 3622cc 16mpg max speed 80mph.

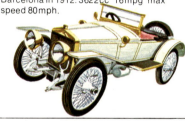

**Lancia Lambda** Between 1922 and 1931 some 13,000 Lambdas in nine different models were produced. The 1922 model had a four cylinder, 2120cc engine capable of 72mph.

**Morris Oxford** Known as the 'bullnose'. When first produced in 1913 it had a four cylinder, 1018cc engine with a top speed of 45mph and cost £175.

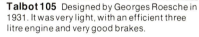

**Rolls Royce Silver Ghost** First produced in 1907, this is the most famous of all Rolls-Royces. Its six cylinder, 7046cc engine produced a top speed of 80mph.

**Talbot 105** Designed by Georges Roesche in 1931. It was very light, with an efficient three litre engine and very good brakes.

**Benelli 750/6** 748cc 4 stroke 45mpg
max 120mph 0–60/*sec overall length
218cm overall width 71cm wheelbase 142cm
weight 220kg

**BMW R60/7** 599cc 4 stroke 58mpg
max 105mph 0–60/7·7sec overall length
213cm overall width 74cm wheelbase 146·5cm
weight 200kg

**BMW R100RS** 980cc 4 stroke 50mpg
max 125mph 0–60/4·5sec overall length
213cm overall width 74cm wheelbase 146·5cm
weight 331kg

**Cossack 175** 173cc 2 stroke 100mpg
max 65mph 0–60/*sec
wheelbase 183cm
weight 109kg

**CZ 471 Deluxe** 246cc 2 stroke 70mpg
max 75mph 0–60/11.3sec wheelbase 132cm
weight 142kg

**Derbi GTS 4** 48·8cc 2 stroke 125mpg
max 47mph overall length 175cm overall
width 83·8cm wheelbase 117cm weight 54kg

**Ducati 860 GTS** 864cc 4 stroke 50mpg
max 120mph 0–60/3·5sec overall length
221cm overall width 71cm wheelbase 150cm
weight 202kg Previously called the KS.

**Dunstall Kawasaki 1000** 1015·9cc 4 stroke
40mpg max 140mph 0–60/*sec wheelbase
160cm weight 238kg Specially built Dunstall
frame with Kawasaki
engine.

**Dunstall Suzuki** 738cc 2 stroke 40mpg max 125mph overall length 222·5cm overall width 87cm wheelbase 149cm weight 213kg

**Fantic Chopper 125** 125cc 2 stroke 60mpg max 75mph 0–60/*sec overall length 210cm overall width *cm wheelbase 143·5cm weight 104kg

**Harley-Davidson FLH 1200 Electra Glide** 1200cc 4 stroke 50mpg max 105mph 0–60/*sec overall length 237·5cm overall width *cm wheelbase 156cm weight 327·5kg

**Honda Camino** 49cc 2 stroke 120mpg max 35mph overall length 165cm overall width 62cm wheelbase 105cm weight 47kg

**Enfield 350 Bullit** 346cc 4 stroke 80mpg max 75mph 0–60/*sec wheelbase 137cm weight 168kg Made in India.

**Harley-Davidson SST 250** 243cc 2 stroke 65mpg max 90mph 0–60/10·9sec overall length 218·5cm overall width 75cm wheelbase 143cm weight 114kg

**Hercules W2000** Wankel engine (294cc) max 100mph weight 159kg

**Honda CB 200** 198cc 4 stroke 60mpg max 80mph 0–60/12·5sec overall length 193·5cm overall width 72cm wheelbase 128·8cm weight 141kg

**Honda CB 750F** 736cc 4 stroke 45mpg max 115mph 0–60/6·2sec overall length 220cm overall width 86cm wheelbase 147cm weight 226kg

**Honda CJ 250 T** 249cc 4 stroke 60mpg max 85mph 0–60/11sec overall length 214·5cm overall width 71cm wheelbase 137·5cm weight 162kg

**Honda GL 1000** 999cc 4 stroke 40mpg max 125mph 0–60/4·8sec overall length 235cm overall width 76cm wheelbase 155cm weight 259kg

**Jawa 350** 343·5cc 2 stroke 70mpg max 84mph wheelbase 135cm weight 157kg

**Kawasaki Z 200** 198cc 4 stroke 95mpg max 80mph 0–60/11sec overall length 198cm overall width 70cm wheelbase 128cm weight 126kg

**Kawasaki Z 1000** 1015cc 4 stroke 45mpg max 130mph 0–60/5sec overall length 224cm overall width 87·4cm wheelbase 150·5cm weight 240kg

**KTM Comet 50RSL** 49cc 2 stroke max 53mph weight 96kg

**Laverda Jota** 980cc 4 stroke 40mpg max 130mph 0–60/13sec overall length 218cm overall width 66cm wheelbase 148cm weight 213kg

**Malaguti Mon Ami** 49cc 2 stroke 120mpg
max 35mph overall length 157cm
overall width 68·5cm wheelbase 103cm
weight 31·8kg

**Moto-Guzzi 850 T3** 844cc 4 stroke
50mpg max 120mph 0–60/4·9sec
overall length 220cm overall width *cm
wheelbase 157cm weight 197kg

**Moto-Guzzi Le Mans** 844cc 4 stroke
40mpg max 125mph 0–60/5sec
overall length 219cm overall width 74cm
wheelbase 157cm weight 242·7kg

**Moto-Guzzi V1000** 948·8cc 4 stroke
40mpg max 110mph 0–60/4·5sec overall
length 221cm overall width *cm wheelbase
157cm weight 254kg

**Moto-Morini Sport 3½** 344cc 4 stroke
50mpg max 95mph 0–60/7·8sec
overall length 203cm overall width 69·5cm
wheelbase 137cm weight 145kg Similar in
appearance to Strada 3½.

**MV Augusta 750 America** 789cc 4 stroke
40mpg max 140mph 0–60/4·9sec
overall length 211cm overall width 72cm
wheelbase 139cm weight 230kg

**MZ TS 250** 243cc 2 stroke 70mpg
max 80mph 0–60/7·8sec
overall length 208cm overall width 63·5cm
wheelbase 132cm
weight 129kg

**Norton Commando Interstate** 828cc
4 stroke 50mpg max 110mph 0–60/5sec
overall length 222cm overall width 66cm
wheelbase 145cm
weight 211kg

**NVT Easy Rider** 49·5cc 2 stroke 130mpg max 30mph overall length 169cm overall width 72cm wheelbase 111cm weight 47kg NVTs are the only mopeds built in Britain.

**Puch Maxi S** 48·8cc 2 stroke 175mpg max 28mph overall length 170cm overall width *cm wheelbase 112cm weight 44kg Several other varieties of Puch mopeds can be seen on the roads.

**Rickman Honda Sports** 750cc 4 stroke 40mpg max 115mph 0–60/6·1sec overall length 206 overall width *cm wheelbase 147cm weight 204kg Rickman Bros. produce specialist bikes.

**Silk 700** 653cc 2 stroke 55mpg max 110mph 0–60/*sec overall length 206cm overall width *cm wheelbase 142cm weight 138kg

**Suzuki GS 750** 748cc 4 stroke 40mpg max 120mph 0–60/6·2sec overall length 222·5cm overall width 87cm wheelbase 149cm weight 223kg

**Suzuki GT 125** 124cc 2 stroke 65mpg max 80mph 0–60/11·5sec overall length 191cm overall width 77cm wheelbase 127cm weight 108kg

**Suzuki GT 250** 247cc 2 stroke 40mpg max 90mph 0–60/9·9sec overall length 204·5cm overall width 81·5cm wheelbase 132cm weight 146kg The top selling 250cc motorcycle in Britain.

**Suzuki RE5** Rotary engine 497cc 30mpg max 105mph 0–60/*sec overall length 222cm overall width *cm wheelbase 150cm weight 230kg

**Triumph Bonneville** 744cc 4 stroke
50mpg max 105mph 0–60/6sec
overall length 222cm overall width 84cm
wheelbase 142cm
weight 179kg

**Triumph Trident T160** 740cc 4 stroke
40mpg max 115mph 0–60/4·9sec
overall length 223·5cm overall width 86cm
wheelbase 147cm weight 228kg

**Vespa 200 Rally** 198cc 2 stroke 94mpg
max 68mph overall length 177cm
overall width *cm wheelbase 123cm
weight 102·75kg

**Yamaha V50P** 49cc 2 stroke 115mpg
max 45mph overall length 184cm
overall width 64·5cm wheelbase 117cm
weight 76kg

**Yamaha RD 250** 247cc 2 stroke 40mpg
max 95mph 0–60/9·1sec overall length
199·5cm overall width 83cm wheelbase
132·5cm weight 150kg RD 400 is similar in
appearance.

**Yamaha XS 750** 747cc 4 stroke 45mpg
max 115mph 0–60/6·2sec
overall length 216cm overall width 89·5cm
wheelbase 146·5cm weight 231kg

**Yamaha XT 500** 499cc 4 stroke 40mpg
max 85mph 0–60/7·5sec overall length
218·5cm overall width 87·5cm wheelbase
142cm weight 140kg

**Zundapp KS 125** 123·6cc 2 stroke *mpg
max 75mph overall length 201cm
overall width *cm wheelbase 132·5cm
weight 110kg

**Routemaster** The red London Transport double decker built by AEC that is famous throughout the world.

**Minibus** There are many minibuses of various types to be seen around the country. This one is a Leyland Redline with a Chorley Coachcraft body.

**Coach** Numerous coaches in a wide variety of designs can be seen on the road. The one shown here is a Duple bodied Bedford of Grey-Green coaches.

**Royal Mail Post bus** In many outlying districts the postman not only delivers letters but also acts as a bus driver. The post bus is used for this dual purpose.

**Open topped bus** A bus very popular at seaside resorts and for use on sight seeing tours. This one is a Leyland Titan PD2 of Merseyside Transport.

**Leyland Fleetline** This type of bus is designed for one man operation. Passengers board the bus by the front door and the centre door is used as an exit only.

**National Coach** Used by the National Coach Company for long distance travel throughout the British Isles.

**Red Arrow** Type of public transport vehicle used for city commuter operation. One of a wide range of buses and coaches used for this purpose.

**London Country Bus** Used by London Country Bus Service and Green Line coaches, this rear-engined bus is designed for one man operation.

**Atlantean** Double-decked, six cylinder, diesel-engined bus produced by British Leyland Truck and Bus Division.

**Foreign Coach** A great many people visit Britain each year so several foreign coaches are on our roads. This is a Fiat with a Van Hool body from Holland.

**Ford Transit**  Commercial transporter designed for medium sized loads. Available in several versions with gross vehicle weights from 2·02 to 3·44 tons.

**Sherpa**  A light transporter van produced by British Leyland. Can be seen in a wide variety of sizes and specifications.

**Chevanne**  Based on the Vauxhall Chevette. It has a 1256cc, 4 cylinder engine with a fuel consumption of 38mpg. Its dimensions are: length 420cm width 157cm height 133cm.

**Ice Cream Van**  A familiar sight on British roads. There are many different types and several makes of ice cream available. All are welcome on a hot summer's day!

**Dumper Truck**  Small truck often seen on construction sites. Used for the transportation of material. The container can be tipped to dispose of the load.

**AA Service Van**  Both the AA and the RAC have patrols throughout Great Britain trained to carry out minor roadside repairs. This is a van of the type used by AA patrolmen.

**AA Relay** Recovery service available to members of the AA who have subscribed to the service. This service was introduced in 1973.

**Taxi** Many modern taxis are just ordinary cars bearing a 'For Hire' sign. There are also specially designed taxis, such as the Austin shown here.

**Pick-Up** A medium sized truck for small loads. This is one of the Ford 'A' Series introduced in 1973. There are several other body types in the same Series.

**RAC Recovery** Service offered by the RAC to ensure that a car and its passengers involved in a breakdown or accident are conveyed home or to their destination.

**Milkfloat**  These are the most common electric vehicles to be seen on the road. Most have a top speed of about 10mph and can carry a load of up to 4cwt.

**Mail Van**  A large number of electric delivery vans can be seen on the road. This Royal Mail Van can go up to 33mph so it can hold its own in city traffic.

**Invalid Chair**  Motorised transport for disabled persons. Some are designed for road use, others you will see on the pavement. Some are used in the home.

**Electric Car**  As yet there is no commercially produced electric car available but as development is progressing well it could be on the roads in the near future.

**Fork Lift Truck**  Not a road vehicle but can be seen occasionally. Used in factories and warehouses for transporting, stacking, and loading goods.

**Gully Cleanser**  Electric vehicle used by many local authorities for the cleaning of drains. Similar vehicles are used for road cleaning operations in many places.

**Road Roller** Used to press down material such as a new road surface. Many people call it a 'steam-roller' but this is wrong as modern machines are powered by diesel.

**JCB** Multi purpose equipment used on construction sites for excavating and levelling the ground.

**5 Ton Truck** An all purpose truck seen in a wide variety of styles and makes. This is one of the 'D' Series manufactured by the Ford Company.

**Tipper Lorry** The rear section of this lorry can be tipped up to an angle of 45° to facilitate unloading.

**Security Van** Often seen outside banks delivering or collecting money. Well protected and manned by trained guards in case of attack from criminals.

**Concrete Mixer** Produces concrete on the way to a construction site. An empty vehicle weighs about 13 tonnes, loaded it weighs in the region of 19 tonnes.

**Closed Lorry** Lorries like this in a variety of styles and makes are used to carry all manner of goods to all parts of the country.

**Artic** Abbreviation of 'Articulated'. The trailer can be detached from the tractor, or cab. Artics can carry longer loads than a normal cab with a trailer.

**Artic and Semi Trailer** An articulated commercial vehicle in which the tractor unit (cab) is completely independent of the trailer.

**Rigid with Trailer** An ordinary rigid truck with a trailer attached to increase the amount that can be transported in a single load.

**Refrigerated Vehicle** Vehicle with a
refrigeration unit and special insulation. Look
for the refrigeration unit mounted at the front
of the body.

**Luton Van** Distinguished by the loading
space above the cab. It is said that these vans
were first used in Luton by local hat
manufacturers.

**Lorry Mounted Crane** Cranes are essential
on building and industrial sites. Some are lorry
mounted like the 30 ton Coles 300T shown
above.

**Low Loader** Often seen with a police escort
because the loads carried are large and heavy.
Others carry less weighty loads, such as
bulldozers, from place to place.

**Horsebox** Specially designed vehicle for the transportation of horses. The larger varieties have a special compartment for the horses' grooms.

**Dump Truck** Used on most building sites for carrying earth and rubble. It is recognisable from the protective headboard that covers the top of the cab.

**Snowplough** Not a regular sight on the roads of the British Isles. Something unusual for you to look out for if you are travelling during the winter months.

**Petrol Tanker** One of a number of such tankers to be seen on the road. They can carry more than 22,700 litres (5000 gallons) of fuel.

**Skip Loader** Carries skips – large containers used for collecting rubbish. You will often see just the skips on a building site awaiting collection.

**Salt Tanker** Similar to the petrol tanker but specially modified for the carrying of chemicals and similar cargos.

**Car Transporter** Can have one or two carrying decks. You may even see one with three decks. Some transporters also have trailers.

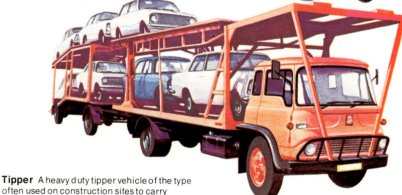

**Tipper** A heavy duty tipper vehicle of the type often used on construction sites to carry rubble and similar loose loads.

**Fire Tender** Fire fighting vehicle carrying a six to eight man crew and a wide range of fire fighting equipment. Some even carry their own water supply.

**Fire Engine** This one has snorkel hydraulic lift equipment. When the lift equipment is raised outriggers extend from the sides of the vehicle to provide stability.

**Ambulance** Used by local authorities for the transportation of the sick and injured. In emergency situations it is usually heard well before it is seen!

**Ambulance** This one belongs to the St. John Ambulance Brigade. On its side is the district to which it belongs.

**Dustcart** Various types of dustcart can be seen. Most of the modern ones have some means of compressing the rubbish.

**Panda** Used for escort duties and local patrol functions. Introduced by Lancashire Police in the late 1960s. Originally dark blue with a white stripe.

**Traffic Patrol Vehicle**  Rover 3500 used by the police for traffic patrol, attending accidents, and similar duties.

**London Transport Car**  Radio control car used by London Transport to monitor and co-ordinate the movement of buses.

**White Liner**  One of the various types of vehicle used by local authorities up and down the country for painting white lines on the road surface.

**Road Sweeper**  These vehicles crawl along the kerbside brushing up the dirt and spraying water to clean the road. The dirt is sucked up into the body of the vehicle.

**Lamp Service Platform**  Mobile platform that can be raised for the maintenance of street lighting, cleaning of road signs, and other roadside operations.

**Drain Cleaner**  Used by local authorities throughout the British Isles for cleaning out roadside drains and private cesspits.

**VW Caravanette** An increasing number of people are driving motorised caravans. They provide a freedom and convenience not available with any other form of travel.

**GP Beach Buggy** The first beach buggy, the Meyers Manx, was designed by Bruce Meyers in America. As they have wide tyres they are easy to handle and very safe to drive.

**Car trailing caravan** A familiar sight on the roads, particularly during the summer months.

**Horse Box** This type of horse box takes only one horse. It is used quite extensively by farmers and private owners.

**Jeep** A popular utility vehicle first created for the use of American servicemen during World War II. Now manufactured by a division of American Motors Corporation.

**Range Rover** V8 cyl 3528cc 20mpg max 99mph length 447cm width 178cm height 178cm Introduced in 1970.

**Land Rover** General Service vehicle with ¾ tonne trailer. Has two or four wheel drive and, with a Rover 2·28 engine, is capable of speeds up to 65 mph.

**Bedford MK** A four tonne Medium Mobility Load Carrier used for carrying general cargo, combat supplies, or troops.

**Foden Tanker** Low Mobility Fuel Tanker capable of carrying 22,500 litres (4950 gallons) of fuel. It is powered by a Rolls Royce Eagle 220 six cylinder diesel engine.

**Cargo Truck** A Low Mobility Load Carrier manufactured by Fodens Ltd. Its unladen weight is 12·48 tonne. Fully laden it is 30·48 tonne, and has a maximum speed of 50 mph.

**Alvis Stalwart** An amphibious load carrier used for general cargo. On land its maximum speed is 39 mph. In still water it can travel at five knots.

**Bedford Coach** 39 seater coach with possible conversion to stretcher ambulance for 12 stretchers. Powered by a 4·9 litre petrol engine it has a maximum speed of 55 mph.

**Scammel Crusader** 22 tonne Low Mobility Tractor Unit with Dyson trailer used for general cargo. The trailer is 955cm long and weighs 27½ tonne when laden.

**Militant Mk 3** An AEC ten ton Medium Mobility Load Carrier used for combat supplies and general cargo. Its six cylinder diesel engine gives it a speed of 52mph.

**Bedford KFA** 3·6 litre, diesel engined Low Mobility Load Carrier with semi-trailer. Used for carrying general cargos.

**Tank Transporter** Used for transporting tanks and other heavy loads. The total length of vehicle and trailer is 1829cm and it is 335cm wide.

# Games to Play in the Car

There are lots of games that can be played in a car to liven up the journey. Here are a few to try.

## When we arrive

Each player takes it in turn to repeat and complete the phrase 'When we arrive at our destination I will visit . . .' But each player must also repeat what everyone has said before adding the place that they will visit. Thus, the longer the game continues the more difficult it becomes to remember what has gone before.

The first player may say 'When we arrive at our destination I will visit the fish and chip shop to buy a bag of chips.' The second player repeats this and adds something else, such as, 'When we arrive at our destination I will visit the fish and chip shop to buy a bag of chips, and the amusement arcade to play on the machines.' The third player adds something else and so the game continues until no-one can remember the correct order of all the things you are going to visit when you arrive at your destination.

## I spy

An old game but still a good one. Each person takes it in turns to say 'I spy something beginning with (a letter of the alphabet)'. The others then have to guess the object, the person who does so being the next to think up an object. Objects chosen must, of course, be visible to everyone.

## Name game

Write down the letters of the alphabet from A to Z and see how many cars you can spot that begin with each letter. The names can be either manufacturers' names or the name given to a particular model.

## Blind estimation

A distant object is chosen and all the passengers in the car have to close their eyes and then shout out when they think the vehicle has reached the object in question. The person who is the nearest wins a point. As the driver must keep his eyes open all the time he can be the judge for this game.

## Registration rigmarole

The registration letters of a passing car are called out and the players have to make up a witty, clever, or absolutely ridiculous sentence using the letters of the registration as the initial letter of each word in the sentence. For example:

GTH  *Granny's teeth hurt*
DFA  *Don't feed alligators*
HAB  *Have a banana*
STC  *Stone the crows*

## Initial collection

This is a variation of the last game, the object being to collect car registrations, the letters of which make a recognisable word or the initials of an organisation, such as BBC, DOG, ITA, SUN. As an extension of this game extra points can be scored by any player that spots a registration that makes a word or a name when the numbers are included, such as MAR 10 (Mario), CUT 1E (Cutie), NAT 10N (Nation), and so on.

**Pub cricket**

Each player looks out for pub signs that depict or mention creatures with legs. For each leg the player scores one point. Thus, *The Duck* will score two points because a duck has two legs; *The Marquis of Salisbury* will also score two; *The Blue Boar* scores four. With some pub names you will have to agree on a specific number of points if the number of legs is open to argument, such as in *The Horse and Hounds*, where only one horse is mentioned (four points) but the number of hounds is not specified. About fifteen points could be given for such signs. The first player to gain a specified number of points (50 or 100) is the winner.

**Coloured cars**

Choose a colour, and the first person to spot a car in that colour wins a point. Ten points wins a game.

Variations on this game can be devised by choosing an animal, the first person to spot the animal either in the flesh or on a hoarding, inn sign, and so on wins the point.

**Spot checks**

Make a long list of some of the items that you might expect to see on your journey. Any player who spots one of the listed items gets a point, and that item is crossed off the list. The person who has the most points when the list is exhausted is the winner.

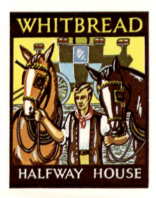

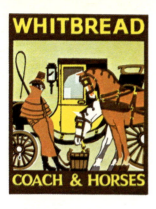

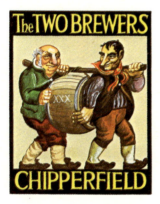

## Back seat bingo

Make some bingo cards (simply a series of squares with numbers in some of the squares). Hand each player a card and a pencil. One person watches the traffic and calls out the last two numbers of as many registration plates as he or she can see. If a player has on his card the number called he crosses it off, and the first to completely clear his card is the winner.

## Sausages

To every question that is asked the victim selected for this game must answer with the single word 'Sausages'. Thus the conversation might proceed as follows:

'*What is your name?*'

'Sausages.'

'*What do you wear on your feet?*'

'Sausages.'

'*What do you like with custard?*'

'Sausages.'

The object of the game is to get the victim to laugh or smile. As soon as he or she does so they are out and someone else has a go and the other players pose questions that they hope will make the victim laugh.

## Animal, vegetable or mineral

This is the old game of 'Twenty Questions'. One person thinks of an object and states whether it is 'animal', 'vegetable' or 'mineral'. The other players are then permitted to ask a total of twenty questions (which can be answered

Some of the pub signs which will score in Pub Cricket.

only by a straightforward 'yes' or 'no'), and then try to guess what the chosen object is. The person who guesses correctly thinks up the next object. If no-one gets the right answer then the same person is allowed another go.

## Alphabetical Lists

Any number of players can participate in this game. The more players there are, the harder the game becomes. First a subject, such as animals, is chosen, and then each player has to name an animal beginning with each subsequent letter of the alphabet. Thus for A one could call aardvark, anteater, ante-

lope, armadillo, and so on. When everyone has named an animal beginning with A you move on to B, and continue thus through the alphabet.

If players are unable to call something beginning with a particular letter then they drop out from the game. The last person remaining in the game is the winner.

Some other possible subjects for the game are: countries, famous people, flowers, fruit, rivers, towns and cities, and vegetables.

Alphabetical lists – animals beginning with D: dinosaur, donkey, dodo, duck, dog, desman, drongo.

# Services & Information

## Tourist boards

For information on places to visit, and current events in particular areas:

*British Tourist Authority*, 64 St James's Street, London, SW1A 1NF.

*Scottish Tourist Board*, 2 Rutland Place, West End, Edinburgh EH1 2YU.

*Wales Tourist Board*, Welcome House, High Street, Llandaff, Cardiff CF5 2YZ.

*Northern Ireland Tourist Board*, River House, High Street, Belfast, and 13 Lower Regent Street, London, S.W.1.

There are, in addition, tourist information offices all over the country which can provide you with a great wealth of local information.

### Publications

*In Britain*. This useful monthly magazine is published by the British Tourist Authority. It contains historical information, places to visit, customs, sporting events and other items of interest to the traveller.

*Historic Houses, Castles and Gardens in Great Britain and Ireland*. This publication will tell you all you need to know about opening times, prices of admission and features of interest (dates of buildings, their architecture etc), about the many houses and gardens open to the public. (Published by ABC Historic Publications).

## Motoring and travellers' organisations

*Automobile Association*, Fanum House, Leicester Square, London WC2H 7LY

*Royal Automobile Club*, 83 Pall Mall, London SW1

*British Caravanners' Club*, 11 Lower Grosvenor Place, London SW1 0EY

*British Cycling Federation*, 26 Park Crescent, London W1N 4BL

*Institute of Advanced Motorists Ltd*, Empire House, Chiswick High Road, London W4 5TJ

*Institute of Motorcycling*, Hartree House, Queensway, London W2 4SQ

*The Transport Trust*, 18 Ramillies Place, London W1V 2BA

## Other useful addresses

*British Waterways Board*, Melbury House, Melbury Terrace, London NW1 6JX.

*Camping Club of Great Britain and Ireland Limited*, 11 Lower Grosvenor Place, London SW1 0EY.

*Caravan Club*, 65 South Molton Street, London W1Y 2AB.

*Inland Waterways Association*, Regent's Park Road, London NW1.

*London Transport Ltd.*, 55 Broadway, London SW1.

*National Garden Scheme*, 57 Lower Belgrave Street, London SW1.

*The National Trust*, 42 Queen Anne's Gate, London SW1.

*The National Trust for Scotland*, 5 Charlotte Square, Edinburgh 2.
*Scotland's Garden Scheme*, 26 Castle Terrace, Edinburgh 1.
*YHA Travel and Services Dept.*, 29 John Adam Street, London WC2.

## Motoring organizations

### Royal Automobile Club (RAC)

The Royal Automobile Club was founded in 1897 as the Automobile Club of Great Britain and Ireland. Ten years later, under the patronage of the Prince of Wales, later Edward VII, it derived its present name. By that time it had already established its first corps of uniformed road patrols and had erected road signs for the benefit of motorists. Many a motorist has been reassured to see the RAC patrol man on his way to provide someone with much needed assistance. The patrol man is not only equipped to carry out automobile repairs, however. He also carries maps, badges, and a first aid kit for he also has to be an adviser, nurse, and policeman as well as a mechanic.

A network of shelter boxes fo patrol men was started in 1913. Si years later the Ascot Traffic Com mittee suggested that it would be a

The AA and RAC badges.

good idea to install a telephone in the shelter hut at Egham, in Surrey. The idea was adopted and the now-familiar RAC telephone box was born. Today more than 1600 such boxes are available to RAC members throughout the British Isles.

**Automobile Association (AA)**

The Automobile Association came into being in 1905 because motorists were being heavily fined for exceeding the speed limit of 20mph. To gain convictions the police hid behind hedges with stop watches, and it was not uncommon for an unsuspecting motorist to collect two or three bookings during a single journey. Eventually police persecution reached such a pitch that a group of motoring enthusiasts formed a band of cyclist scouts who would warn motorists if a speed trap was in operation. From this grew the idea of forming a more permanent organization to protect the interests of motorists, and the Automobile Association was born.

Today both organizations offer invaluable aid and advice to the motorist. In addition to the familiar patrol vans, providing technical assistance to the motorist, both organizations provide a wealth of other services for their members. These include a special 'get you home' breakdown service, arranging insurance, the erection of signposts and notices, and the provision of information and advice on a wide variety of subjects of interest and importance to the motorist.

# RAC young driver course

In order to prepare young people for the responsibilities they will have to face as road users the RAC runs a young driver course. This is organized and controlled by the RAC in conjunction with schools and colleges around the country.

Tuition includes both theoretical and practical work designed to provide a thorough training in all aspects of road safety and car driving. The course covers the highway code road manners, car control, night driving, self-help breakdown mechanics, and many other aspects of driving. The purpose of the course is to educate young people into the correct attitudes towards driving even before they are old enough to drive.

The pupil is given at least eleven hours instruction at the wheel of a car if he or she is over seventeen years of age. If the pupil is under seventeen arrangements can usually be made to give some driving tuition off the public highway, for example on an old airfield.

At the end of the course the pupil is given both a written and a practical test set by the RAC. Successful students receive a Certificate of Achievement. This does not, of course, entitle them to drive a car on the public roads. It does, however, give them useful experience that will serve them in good stead when they decide to take the official driving test.

# Fact Finder

## Principal lakes in the United Kingdom

The first figures given are in square kilometres; square miles are shown in brackets.

### England
| | | |
|---|---|---|
| Bassenthwaite, Cumbria | 5·4 | (2·1) |
| Derwentwater, Cumbria | 5·4 | (2·1) |
| Coniston Water, Cumbria | 4·9 | (1·9) |
| Ullswater, Cumbria | 8·8 | (3·4) |
| Lake Windermere, Cumbria | 25·9 | (10) |

### Scotland
| | | |
|---|---|---|
| Loch Awe, Strathclyde | 38·8 | (15) |
| Loch Lomond, Strathclyde/Central | 71 | (27·5) |
| Loch Ness, Highland | 57 | (22) |

### Wales
| | | |
|---|---|---|
| Lake Bala, Gwynedd | 9·6 | (3·7) |
| Lake Vyrnwy, Powys | 8·3 | (3·2) |

### Northern Ireland
| | | |
|---|---|---|
| Lower Lough Erne, Fermanagh | 104·9 | (40·5) |
| Lough Neagh, Antrim/Armagh/Down/ Londonderry/Tyrone | 381 | (147) |

## Areas of the United Kingdom

The first figures given are in square kilometres; square miles are shown in brackets.

| | Land | Inland non-tidal water | Total area |
|---|---|---|---|
| England | 129,635 (50,054) | 725 (280) | 130,360 (50,334) |
| Scotland | 77,174 (29,798) | 1,596 (616) | 78,770 (30,414) |
| Wales | 20,639 (7,969) | 124 (48) | 20,763 (8,017) |
| Northern Ireland | 13,483 (5,206) | 637 (246) | 14,120 (5,452) |
| United Kingdom | 240,931 (93,027) | 3,082 (1,190) | 244,013 (94,217) |

Thirlmere, a lake 6 km (4 miles) long, in Cumbria.

## Principal rivers in the United Kingdom

The first figures given are in kilometres; miles are shown in brackets.

| River | Source | Flows to | Length |
|-------|--------|----------|--------|
| **England** | | | |
| Great Ouse | Brackley, Northamptonshire | The Wash | 250 (156) |
| Severn | Plynlimon, Powys | Bristol Channel | 352 (220) |
| Thames | Lechlade, Gloucestershire | North Sea | 336 (210) |
| Trent | Biddulph Moor, Staffordshire | River Ouse | 272 (170) |
| **Scotland** | | | |
| Clyde | Earncraig, Strathclyde | Firth of Clyde | 170 (106) |
| Spey | Loch Spey, Highland | Moray Firth | 171 (107) |
| Tay | Beinn Oss, Tayside | Firth of Tay | 187 (117) |
| **Wales** | | | |
| Wye | Plynlimon, Dyfed | River Severn | 208 (130) |

## Highest mountains in the United Kingdom

The first figures given are in metres; feet are shown in brackets.

**England**

| | |
|---|---|
| Helvellyn, Cumbria | 950 (3,116) |
| Scafell, Cumbria | 964 (3,162) |
| Scafell Pike, Cumbria | 978 (3,210) |
| Skiddaw, Cumbria | 931 (3,052) |

**Scotland**

| | |
|---|---|
| Braeriach, Grampian | 1,295 (4,246) |
| Ben Macdhui, Grampian | 1,311 (4,296) |
| Ben Nevis, Highland | 1,343 (4,404) |
| Cairn Toul, Grampian | 1,293 (4,240) |

**Wales**

| | |
|---|---|
| Carnedd Dafydd, Gwynedd | 1,044 (3,424) |
| Carnedd Llewelyn, Gwynedd | 1,062 (3,484) |
| Glyder Fawr, Gwynedd | 999 (3,277) |
| Snowdon, Gwynedd | 1,085 (3,560) |

**Northern Ireland**

| | |
|---|---|
| Slieve Donard, Down | 852 (2,795) |

The Helford River in Cornwall, although
not a principal river, is one of the prettiest
in England.

Principal rivers, lakes and mountains in
the United Kingdom.

NORTH WEST HIGHLANDS

Spey

Loch
Ness

Braeriach
Ben Nevis
1347m
Ben Macdhui
Cairn Toul

GRAMPIANS

Loch
Awe

Tay

Loch
Lomond

Clyde

Tweed

SOUTHERN UPLANDS

Tyne

DERRYVEAGH
MOUNTAINS

Bann

Sca Fell
978m

Derwentwater

Lough
Neagh

Bassenthwaite

Ullswater

Lough
Erne

Coniston
Water

Windermere

MOURNE MTS.

Slieve
Donard
852m

PENNINES

Mersey

Trent

Snowdon
1085m

Dee

Lake Bala

Lake Vyrnwy

CAMBRIAN MTS.

Severn

Avon

Ouse

Wye

BRECON
BEACONS

Thames

EXMOOR

Land over 400m

DARTMOOR

## Conversion Tables

The figures in the central column for each of the conversion tables represent the equivalent values for the figures in the columns on the left and right. For example, 1 kilometre equals 0·621 miles, and 1 mile equals 1·609 kilometres. So by looking in the column for the conversion you want, you can read off the correct figure immediately. For combinations other than shown, simply add or multiply any of the given conversions to arrive at the correct figure, for example, 16 gallons equals 72·736 litres (45·460 + 27·276 litres).

| Distance conversion | | | Liquid conversion | | |
|---|---|---|---|---|---|
| Miles | Kilometres or miles | Kilometres | Gallons | Litres or gallons | Litres |
| 0·621 | 1 | 1·609 | 0·220 | 1 | 4·546 |
| 1·243 | 2 | 3·219 | 0·440 | 2 | 9·092 |
| 1·864 | 3 | 4·828 | 0·660 | 3 | 13·638 |
| 2·486 | 4 | 6·437 | 0·880 | 4 | 18·184 |
| 3·107 | 5 | 8·047 | 1·100 | 5 | 22·730 |
| 3·728 | 6 | 9·656 | 1·320 | 6 | 27·276 |
| 4·350 | 7 | 11·265 | 1·540 | 7 | 31·822 |
| 4·971 | 8 | 12·875 | 1·760 | 8 | 36·368 |
| 5·592 | 9 | 14·484 | 1·980 | 9 | 40·914 |
| 6·214 | 10 | 16·093 | 2·200 | 10 | 45·460 |
| 15·534 | 25 | 40·234 | 4·400 | 20 | 90·919 |
| 31·069 | 50 | 80·467 | 5·500 | 25 | 113·649 |
| 46·603 | 75 | 120·701 | 10·999 | 50 | 227·298 |
| 62·137 | 100 | 160·934 | 21·998 | 100 | 454·596 |

### Conversion tables for petrol consumption

| Miles per gallon | 10 | 11 | 12 | 13 | 14 | 15 | 16 | 17 | 18 | 19 |
|---|---|---|---|---|---|---|---|---|---|---|
| Kilometres per litre | 3·5 | 3·9 | 4·2 | 4·6 | 5·0 | 5·3 | 5·7 | 6·0 | 6·4 | 6·7 |
| Miles per gallon | 20 | 21 | 22 | 23 | 24 | 25 | 30 | 35 | 40 | 45 |
| Kilometres per litre | 7·1 | 7·4 | 7·8 | 8·1 | 8·5 | 8·8 | 10·6 | 12·4 | 14·2 | 15·9 |

# What's in a name?

It is an interesting game whilst on a journey to try to discover how the places through which you travel first obtained their names. Many of the places through which you pass will have names that derive from old English, Danish, French, or Latin – some are reminders of the many people who have conquered these islands in years gone by.

The majority of English place names describe the area as it once existed. Examples of this type of name are Plumstead – the place where plums grow; Oxford – the ford for oxen; and Stonebridge – which means exactly what it says.

To study the derivation of all the names you will come across would take many years of dedicated study, but you can gain a good idea of the name's source by looking at the list given below which tells you the original meaning of many of the words that you will find in modern place names. From this list you should be able to deduce that Lancaster was originally a Roman settlement, as the latter part of the names comes from *castra* the Latin for camp. There was probably a fort at Canterbury as *bury* comes from the old English word for a town or a fort. In actual fact Canterbury means the fort of the Cantware (people of Kent). Kirkham is obviously so called because it originally consisted of a church (kirk) within or belonging to a village (ham).

Without either a good knowledge of old languages or of the region through which you are passing, you may be unlikely to find the exact derivation but you will in many instances be able to get a good idea of how the name was formed.

| Word | Meaning | Example |
|------|---------|---------|
| Aber | river mouth | Aberdovey |
| Barrow, Berry | hill, mound | Barrowby |
| Barton | hill town | Barton upon Humber |
| Beck | stream | Birbeck |
| Berwick | marsh town | Berwick |
| Bold, Bootle | building | Bootle |
| Bottom | valley bottom | Bottomstead |
| Botham | valley bottom | Bothamstall |
| Bridge | bridge | Bridgehampton |
| Brock, Brook, Brough | stream | Brockhampton |
| Brough, Burgh | fortified place | Wellingborough |
| Bourne, Burn | spring, stream | Bournemouth |
| By | farmstead | Derby |

| Camp | field | Warningcamp |
|---|---|---|
| Caster, Cester, Chester | Roman fortification, camp | Doncaster |
| Church | church | Churchstow |
| Cleve, Cliffe, Cliff | cliff | Clevedon |
| Coat, Cote | cottage | Coatham |
| Cross | cross | Crosby |
| Dale | valley, dale | Edale |
| Dean, Den | wooded valley | Deanham |
| Ditch, Dyke | ditch, dyke | Ditchampton |
| Fleet | estuary, stream | Fleetham |
| Ford | ford | Bedford |
| Ham | homestead, village | Birmingham |
| Hampton | home farm | Brockhampton |
| Hay | piece of enclosed land | Harthay |
| Head | headland | Beachy Head |
| Hol, Hole | hollow | Hoole |
| Holm, Holme | small island | Oxenholme |
| Hop, Hope | small valley | Longhope |
| Hoe, Hough | spur of a hill | Ivinghoe |
| Hirst, Hurst | wood | Templehurst |
| Hithe | port, haven | Rotherhithe |
| Kel, Keld | spring | Keldholme |
| Kirk | church | Ormskirk |
| Lea, Lee, Leigh | meadow | Leigh-on-Sea |
| Llan | church | Llandaff |
| Mear, Mere | lake | Grasmere |
| Minster, Mister | monastery, church | Southminster |
| Mouth | river mouth | Tynemouth |
| Nas, Naze, Nes | headland, cape | Walton on the Naze |
| Pen | headland, cape | Penzance |
| Port | port | Gosport |
| Shat, Shot | strip of land | Bagshot |
| Shaw | copse | Shawbury |
| Slade, Sled | valley | Sledmere |
| Stead | place, religious place | Hemel Hempstead |
| Stock, Stoke | stockaded place | Stoke Poges |
| Stowe | stockaded place | Felixstowe |
| Thorpe, Throp | village | Langthorpe |
| Thwaite | clearing | Braithwaite |
| Toft | homestead | Lowestoft |

| Tor | rock | Haytor |
| Ton, Tone | village | Hazelton |
| Wade | ford | Biggleswade |
| Wel, Well, Wal, Wall | well, spring | Blackwell |
| Wick, Wich, Wig | marsh, village | Keswick |
| Worth | enclosure | Tamworth |

## Roads in the United Kingdom

*(Figures as at June 1976)*

**England, Scotland and Wales**

| | kilometres | miles |
| --- | --- | --- |
| Motorways | 2,225 | 1,382 |
| Principal roads | 33,000 | 20,500 |
| Other roads | 296,000 | 183,830 |
| Total | 331,225 | 205,712 |

**Northern Ireland**

| | kilometres | miles |
| --- | --- | --- |
| Trunk roads | 636 | 395 |
| Class I | 1,663 | 1,033 |
| Class II | 2,834 | 1,760 |
| Unclassified | 13,369 | 8,304 |
| Total | 18,502 | 11,492 |

## A licence to drive

Every driver of a mechanically powered vehicle must, by law, be in possession of a certificate of competence to drive that class of vehicle.

When driving licences were first issued following the Motor Car Act of 1903 it was not necessary to prove that one was capable of driving. The car owner simply paid the required fee to the local authority or borough council and a driving permit was issued. In 1930 it became necessary for anyone with a physical disability to first pass a test before he or she was issued with a licence. Four years later this requirement was extended to include all new drivers. There are now over twenty million people in the United Kingdom who hold a driving licence, but there are still some drivers who have never taken a test because their licence was issued prior to 1934.

About 1,750,000 people take the test each year. Of this number less than half pass first time.

Learner drivers are issued with a *provisional* licence which allows them to drive on the public highway provided that they are accompanied and supervised by someone holding a full licence. A learner driver must also display L plates at the front and the rear of the vehicle he is driving. This remains the case until he has passed the driving test, which lasts approximately 30 minutes, under the scrutiny of a qualified examiner.

To attain the full licence the driver must show that he has attained the required level of driving ability and that he can drive without danger to other road users. He is also required to show a knowledge of the Highway Code, the book of rules and regulations that covers road use. In addition he must prove that he can read a car number plate at a distance of 22·86 metres (25 yards) to show that he has reasonable eyesight. Spectacles may be worn to read the number plate in the test, but it is an offence for a driver who needs spectacles not to wear them whilst he is driving. Failure to wear spectacles could result in the driver losing his licence for a period of time.

Some of the other offences for which a driver may lose his licence are speeding, driving without due care and attention, ignoring a traffic signal, and dangerous driving.

## Road distances – Ireland

These distances are based on principal road routes. They are not, therefore, always the shortest distance between any two places.

A road in the Mourne Mountains, Northern Ireland.

| | Antrim | Athlone | Belfast | Cork | Dublin | Dundalk | Enniskillen | Galway | Kilkenny | Killarney | Larne | Limerick | Londonderry | Sligo | Waterford | Wexford | Wicklow |
|---|---|---|---|---|---|---|---|---|---|---|---|---|---|---|---|---|---|
| Antrim | | | | | | | | | | | | | | | | | |
| Athlone | 140 | | | | | | | | | | | | | | | | |
| Belfast | 17 | 139 | | | | | | | | | | | | | | | |
| Cork | 271 | 131 | 265 | | | | | | | | | | | | | | |
| Dublin | 112 | 77 | 104 | 161 | | | | | | | | | | | | | |
| Dundalk | 60 | 94 | 52 | 213 | 52 | | | | | | | | | | | | |
| Enniskillen | 83 | 88 | 87 | 217 | 107 | 64 | | | | | | | | | | | |
| Galway | 189 | 56 | 195 | 125 | 133 | 143 | 118 | | | | | | | | | | |
| Kilkenny | 186 | 75 | 178 | 90 | 74 | 126 | 148 | 103 | | | | | | | | | |
| Killarney | 280 | 140 | 279 | 54 | 189 | 234 | 228 | 130 | 120 | | | | | | | | |
| Larne | 22 | 160 | 21 | 286 | 125 | 73 | 108 | 216 | 199 | 300 | | | | | | | |
| Limerick | 213 | 73 | 212 | 62 | 122 | 167 | 161 | 63 | 69 | 67 | 233 | | | | | | |
| Londonderry | 60 | 149 | 77 | 280 | 149 | 100 | 63 | 172 | 211 | 291 | 77 | 224 | | | | | |
| Sligo | 125 | 71 | 129 | 202 | 134 | 106 | 42 | 84 | 146 | 211 | 150 | 144 | 88 | | | | |
| Waterford | 216 | 105 | 208 | 75 | 104 | 156 | 178 | 141 | 30 | 119 | 229 | 78 | 241 | 176 | | | |
| Wexford | 209 | 114 | 201 | 113 | 97 | 149 | 193 | 154 | 50 | 157 | 222 | 116 | 246 | 185 | 38 | | |
| Wicklow | 144 | 109 | 136 | 165 | 32 | 84 | 139 | 165 | 102 | 209 | 157 | 171 | 181 | 166 | 90 | 69 | |

# Road distances – Great Britain

These distances are based on principal road routes. They are not, therefore, always the shortest distance between any two places.

Aberdeen Harbour.

| | Aberdeen | Aberystwyth | Birmingham | Bristol | Cambridge | Canterbury | Cardiff | Darlington | Doncaster | Dover | Edinburgh | Fishguard | Glasgow | Harwich | Holyhead | Inverness | Leeds |
|---|---|---|---|---|---|---|---|---|---|---|---|---|---|---|---|---|---|
| Aberdeen | | | | | | | | | | | | | | | | | |
| Aberystwyth | 450 | | | | | | | | | | | | | | | | |
| Birmingham | 409 | 120 | | | | | | | | | | | | | | | |
| Bristol | 490 | 128 | 82 | | | | | | | | | | | | | | |
| Cambridge | 461 | 220 | 100 | 145 | | | | | | | | | | | | | |
| Canterbury | 559 | 270 | 169 | 180 | 112 | | | | | | | | | | | | |
| Cardiff | 492 | 110 | 101 | 44 | 180 | 220 | | | | | | | | | | | |
| Darlington | 263 | 232 | 168 | 250 | 197 | 287 | 282 | | | | | | | | | | |
| Doncaster | 343 | 175 | 96 | 179 | 119 | 216 | 197 | 72 | | | | | | | | | |
| Dover | 574 | 285 | 184 | 195 | 127 | 15 | 239 | 303 | 231 | | | | | | | | |
| Edinburgh | 123 | 327 | 286 | 367 | 338 | 436 | 365 | 140 | 220 | 451 | | | | | | | |
| Fishguard | 494 | 56 | 176 | 156 | 271 | 332 | 112 | 288 | 236 | 335 | 383 | | | | | | |
| Glasgow | 150 | 326 | 285 | 366 | 352 | 452 | 378 | 168 | 236 | 467 | 45 | 369 | | | | | |
| Harwich | 527 | 286 | 166 | 195 | 66 | 111 | 223 | 263 | 191 | 126 | 404 | 331 | 418 | | | | |
| Holyhead | 430 | 113 | 153 | 211 | 243 | 319 | 212 | 222 | 180 | 334 | 304 | 169 | 303 | 309 | | | |
| Inverness | 105 | 482 | 445 | 528 | 497 | 595 | 524 | 299 | 379 | 601 | 159 | 529 | 176 | 563 | 463 | | |
| Leeds | 322 | 173 | 111 | 206 | 148 | 254 | 212 | 59 | 28 | 269 | 199 | 229 | 210 | 214 | 163 | 358 | |
| Liverpool | 334 | 104 | 94 | 164 | 184 | 263 | 164 | 134 | 86 | 278 | 210 | 160 | 211 | 250 | 94 | 376 | 74 |
| London | 501 | 212 | 111 | 114 | 52 | 58 | 155 | 230 | 158 | 73 | 378 | 262 | 394 | 71 | 261 | 537 | 190 |
| Newcastle | 230 | 270 | 209 | 295 | 231 | 329 | 310 | 33 | 113 | 344 | 107 | 326 | 143 | 297 | 260 | 266 | 92 |
| Norwich | 487 | 267 | 155 | 221 | 60 | 154 | 237 | 216 | 144 | 169 | 364 | 331 | 380 | 63 | 299 | 523 | 174 |
| Nottingham | 388 | 154 | 50 | 132 | 84 | 181 | 152 | 117 | 45 | 196 | 265 | 210 | 278 | 150 | 172 | 424 | |
| Penzance | 683 | 313 | 268 | 186 | 329 | 339 | 230 | 436 | 365 | 354 | 560 | 342 | 559 | 353 | 397 | 720 | 381 |
| Plymouth | 614 | 244 | 199 | 117 | 260 | 270 | 161 | 367 | 296 | 285 | 491 | 273 | 490 | 284 | 328 | 652 | 312 |
| Portsmouth | 546 | 223 | 137 | 96 | 131 | 120 | 140 | 297 | 225 | 128 | 423 | 252 | 422 | 145 | 286 | 584 | 251 |
| Salisbury | 533 | 179 | 113 | 52 | 139 | 141 | 96 | 283 | 201 | 156 | 400 | 208 | 399 | 155 | 263 | 559 | 227 |
| Southampton | 530 | 202 | 128 | 75 | 136 | 136 | 119 | 281 | 209 | 149 | 416 | 231 | 415 | 150 | 283 | 575 | 235 |
| Stranraer | 235 | 342 | 301 | 382 | 368 | 468 | 384 | 182 | 250 | 483 | 133 | 385 | 85 | 434 | 321 | 259 | 224 |
| Swansea | 506 | 76 | 126 | 85 | 216 | 261 | 41 | 288 | 222 | 280 | 383 | 71 | 382 | 261 | 189 | 512 | 229 |
| York | 309 | 197 | 134 | 215 | 157 | 254 | 242 | 16 | 38 | 269 | 186 | 253 | 211 | 223 | 187 | 313 | 24 |

172

# Vehicles licensed in Great Britain

The roads of the British Isles become more congested each year as more and more vehicles use them. It is estimated that by the year 2000 there will be nearly 30,000,000 motor vehicles in use – almost twice as many as there are now!

The table below shows how the numbers have risen since 1955.

| Year | Motor cars | Motor cycles | Taxis, buses, & coaches | Goods vehicles | Other vehicles | Total |
|---|---|---|---|---|---|---|
| 1955 | 3,610,000 | 1,277,000 | 107,000 | 1,134,000 | 442,000 | 6,570,000 |
| 1965 | 9,132,000 | 1,739,000 | 99,000 | 1,644,000 | 648,000 | 13,262,000 |
| 1970 | 11,802,000 | 1,160,000 | 105,000 | 1,659,000 | 596,000 | 15,322,000 |
| 1975 | 14,060,000 | 1,280,000 | 114,000 | 1,812,000 | 605,000 | 17,871,000 |
| 1978 | 13,992,000 | 1,202,000 | 112,000 | 1,691,000 | 657,000 | 17,654,000 |

## Vehicles licensed in Northern Ireland

| Year | Motor cars | Motor cycles | Taxis, buses & coaches | Goods vehicles | Other vehicles | Total |
|---|---|---|---|---|---|---|
| 1978 | 338,000 | 17,000 | 2,000 | 39,000 | 20,000 | 416,000 |

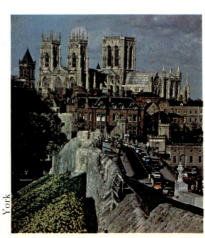

York Minster from the City Walls.

| | Newcastle | Norwich | Nottingham | Penzance | Plymouth | Portsmouth | Salisbury | Southampton | Stranraer | Swansea |
|---|---|---|---|---|---|---|---|---|---|---|
| Norwich | 257 | | | | | | | | | |
| Nottingham | 158 | 123 | | | | | | | | |
| Penzance | 481 | 389 | 318 | | | | | | | |
| Plymouth | 412 | 320 | 249 | 78 | | | | | | |
| Portsmouth | 338 | 181 | 179 | 243 | 174 | | | | | |
| Salisbury | 324 | 189 | 165 | 199 | 130 | 44 | | | | |
| Southampton | 322 | 186 | 163 | 222 | 153 | 21 | 23 | | | |
| Stranraer | 163 | 396 | 294 | 575 | 506 | 438 | 415 | 422 | | |
| Swansea | 321 | 273 | 176 | 271 | 202 | 181 | 137 | 160 | 398 | |
| York | 79 | 182 | 83 | 401 | 332 | 262 | 234 | 247 | 225 | 260 |

# Where is it registered?

All motor vehicles are required by law to carry a registration plate. This has to be displayed at the front and at the rear of the vehicle. The plate is allocated to the vehicle when it is new and, in most cases, it retains that plate whilst it remains licensed.

By looking at the plates on cars and other motor vehicles it is possible to say in what part of the country it was originally registered. It is also possible to discover some other interesting facts about the vehicle, simply by looking at its registration plate.

Registration plates first came into force in 1904 and, as there were only comparatively few cars on the road at the time, consisted of only one or two letters and a single number. Each licensing authority was allocated a particular letter, or two-letter combination, and these were used with the numbers 1 to 99. As motor travel became more within the reach of the ordinary man in the street it soon proved necessary to increase the numbers available, and they were extended up to 9999.

By 1932 there were so many vehicles on the road that the system of one or two letters followed by up to four numbers was inadequate. To overcome the problem it was decided to extend the letter prefixes to include up to three letters. Twenty-one years later, in 1953, the system was expanded even further by allowing licensing authorities to put the numbers in front of the letters. Thus the number ABC 123 would have belonged to a completely different vehicle to 123 ABC. Within ten years it was found that many councils were beginning to use up all the numbers available to them under this system, and so a seven-symbol registration system was introduced. This consists of three letters and up to three numbers followed by a suffix letter to indicate the year of registration. By looking at these suffixes it is possible to tell in which year a car was registered. Thus, a vehicle with the letter N after the numbers was registered between 1st August, 1974 and the 31st July, 1975.

In addition to the year of licence, it is also possible to establish the original licensing authority for the vehicle. This is done as follows: if there is only one letter on the registration plate look that letter up in the table on the following pages and you will discover where the vehicle was originally registered. The same applies for a two-letter registration – look up the two letters in the table. The procedure for a three-letter registration is slightly different. In this case you ignore the first letter and look up the last two. Thus in the case of the letters ELD, ignore the E and look up LD and you will find that the vehicle was originally registered in Greater London.

In some cases this system will not be accurate because of the practice in recent years of driver's transferring licence numbers from vehicle to vehicle so that they have a number that forms their initials, a word associated with their job, and so on. Such numbers are, however, interesting in their own right for they may give an indication of the driver's name or profession. Next time you go collecting car numbers see how many you can spot that form a name or which are obviously the initials of the driver.

If you ever see a car that has no registration number it belongs to the Queen. These are the only cars that do not have registration plates.

| Licensing Authority | Registration letter |
|---|---|
| Salisbury | AA |
| Worcester | AB |
| Coventry | AC |
| Gloucester | AD |
| Bristol | AE |
| Truro | AF |
| Hull | AG |
| Norwich | AH |
| Middlesbrough | AJ |
| Sheffield | AK |
| Nottingham | AL |
| Swindon | AM |
| Reading | AN |
| Carlisle | AO |
| Brighton | AP |
| Chelmsford | AR |
| Inverness | AS |
| Hull | AT |
| Nottingham | AU |
| Peterborough | AV |
| Shrewsbury | AW |
| Cardiff | AX |
| Leicester | AY |
| Manchester | BA |
| Newcastle-upon-Tyne | BB |
| Leicester | BC |
| Northampton | BD |
| Grimsby | BE |
| Stoke-on-Trent | BF |
| Liverpool | BG |
| Luton | BH |
| Ipswich | BJ |
| Portsmouth | BK |
| Reading | BL |
| Luton | BM |
| Bolton | BN |
| Cardiff | BO |
| Portsmouth | BP |
| Durham | BR |
| Kirkwall | BS |
| York | BT |
| Manchester | BU |
| Preston | BV |
| Oxford | BW |
| Haverfordwest | BX |
| London NW | BY |
| Chester | CA |
| Bolton | CB |
| Bangor | CC |
| Brighton | CD |
| Cambridge | CE |

| | | | | |
|---|---|---|---|---|
| Reading | CF | Sheffield | DT |
| Salisbury | CG | Coventry | DU |
| Nottingham | CH | Exeter | DV |
| Hereford | CJ | Cardiff | DW |
| Preston | CK | Ipswich | DX |
| Norwich | CL | Hastings | DY |
| Liverpool | CM | | |
| Newcastle-upon-Tyne | CN | Dudley | EA |
| Plymouth | CO | Cambridge | EB |
| Huddersfield | CP | Kendal | EC |
| Portsmouth | CR | Warrington | ED |
| Ayr | CS | Grimsby | EE |
| Boston | CT | Middlesbrough | EF |
| Newcastle-upon-Tyne | CU | Peterborough | EG |
| Truro | CV | Stoke-on-Trent | EH |
| Preston | CW | Aberystwyth | EJ |
| Huddersfield | CX | Warrington | EK |
| Swansea | CY | Bournemouth | EL |
| | | Liverpool | EM |
| Birmingham | DA | Bolton | EN |
| Manchester | DB | Barrow-in-Furness | EO |
| Middlesbrough | DC | Swansea | EP |
| Gloucester | DD | Cambridge | ER |
| Haverfordwest | DE | Dundee | ES |
| Gloucester | DF | Sheffield | ET |
| Gloucester | DG | Bristol | EU |
| Dudley | DH | Chelmsford | EV |
| Warrington | DJ | Peterborough | EW |
| Bolton | DK | Norwich | EX |
| Newport (IoW) | DL | Bangor | EY |
| Chester | DM | Stoke-on-Trent | FA |
| York | DN | Bristol | FB |
| Boston | DO | Oxford | FC |
| Reading | DP | Dudley | FD |
| Plymouth | DR | Lincoln | FE |
| Glasgow | DS | Aberystwyth | FF |

| Place | Code | Place | Code |
|---|---|---|---|
| Brighton | **FG** | London SE | **GU** |
| Gloucester | **FH** | Ipswich | **GV** |
| Exeter | **FJ** | London SE | **GW** |
| Dudley | **FK** | London SE | **GX** |
| Peterborough | **FL** | London SE | **GY** |
| Chester | **FM** | | |
| Canterbury | **FN** | Dudley | **HA** |
| Hereford | **FO** | Cardiff | **HB** |
| Leicester | **FP** | Hastings | **HC** |
| Preston | **FR** | Huddersfield | **HD** |
| Edinburgh | **FS** | Sheffield | **HE** |
| Newcastle-upon-Tyne | **FT** | Liverpool | **HF** |
| Grimsby | **FU** | Preston | **HG** |
| Preston | **FV** | Carlisle | **HH** |
| Lincoln | **FW** | Chelmsford | **HJ** |
| Bournemouth | **FX** | Chelmsford | **HK** |
| Liverpool | **FY** | Sheffield | **HL** |
| | | London C | **HM** |
| Glasgow | **GA** | Middlesbrough | **HN** |
| Glasgow | **GB** | Salisbury | **HO** |
| London SW | **GC** | Coventry | **HP** |
| Glasgow | **GD** | Swindon | **HR** |
| Glasgow | **GE** | Glasgow | **HS** |
| London SW | **GF** | Bristol | **HT** |
| Glasgow | **GG** | Bristol | **HU** |
| London SW | **GH** | London C | **HV** |
| London SW | **GJ** | Bristol | **HW** |
| London SW | **GK** | London C | **HX** |
| Truro | **GL** | Bristol | **HY** |
| Reading | **GM** | | |
| London SW | **GN** | Manchester | **JA** |
| London SW | **GO** | Reading | **JB** |
| London SW | **GP** | Bangor | **JC** |
| Durham | **GR** | London C | **JD** |
| Luton | **GS** | Cambridge | **JE** |
| London SW | **GT** | Leicester | **JF** |

| Place | Code | Place | Code |
|---|---|---|---|
| Canterbury | **JG** | Sheffield | **KU** |
| Reading | **JH** | Coventry | **KV** |
| Canterbury | **JJ** | Sheffield | **KW** |
| Hastings | **JK** | Luton | **KX** |
| Boston | **JL** | Sheffield | **KY** |
| Reading | **JM** | | |
| Chelmsford | **JN** | London NW | **LA** |
| Oxford | **JO** | London NW | **LB** |
| Warrington | **JP** | London NW | **LC** |
| Newcastle-upon-Tyne | **JR** | London NW | **LD** |
| Stornoway | **JS** | London NW | **LE** |
| Bournemouth | **JT** | London NW | **LF** |
| Leicester | **JU** | Chester | **LG** |
| Grimsby | **JV** | London NW | **LH** |
| Birmingham | **JW** | Bournemouth | **LJ** |
| Huddersfield | **JX** | London NW | **LK** |
| Plymouth | **JY** | London NW | **LL** |
| | | London NW | **LM** |
| Liverpool | **KA** | London NW | **LN** |
| Liverpool | **KB** | London NW | **LO** |
| Liverpool | **KC** | London NW | **LP** |
| Liverpool | **KD** | London NW | **LR** |
| Maidstone | **KE** | Stirling | **LS** |
| Liverpool | **KF** | London NW | **LT** |
| Cardiff | **KG** | London NW | **LU** |
| Hull | **KH** | Liverpool | **LV** |
| Maidstone | **KJ** | London NW | **LW** |
| Maidstone | **KK** | London NW | **LX** |
| Maidstone | **KL** | London NW | **LY** |
| Maidstone | **KM** | | |
| Maidstone | **KN** | Chester | **MA** |
| Maidstone | **KO** | Chester | **MB** |
| Maidstone | **KP** | London NE | **MC** |
| Maidstone | **KR** | London NE | **MD** |
| Selkirk | **KS** | London NE | **ME** |
| Canterbury | **KT** | London NE | **MF** |

| Location | Code | Location | Code |
|---|---|---|---|
| London NE | MG | Nottingham | NU |
| London NE | MH | Northampton | NV |
| Luton | MJ | Leeds | NW |
| London NE | MK | Dudley | NX |
| London NE | ML | Cardiff | NY |
| London NE | MM | | |
| (not used) | MN | Birmingham | OA |
| Reading | MO | Birmingham | OB |
| London NE | MP | Birmingham | OC |
| Swindon | MR | Exeter | OD |
| Stirling | MS | Birmingham | OE |
| London NE | MT | Birmingham | OF |
| London NE | MU | Birmingham | OG |
| London SE | MV | Birmingham | OH |
| Swindon | MW | Birmingham | OJ |
| London SE | MX | Birmingham | OK |
| London SE | MY | Birmingham | OL |
| | | Birmingham | OM |
| Manchester | NA | Birmingham | ON |
| Manchester | NB | Chelmsford | OO |
| Manchester | NC | Birmingham | OP |
| Manchester | ND | Portsmouth | OR |
| Manchester | NE | Stranraer | OS |
| Manchester | NF | Portsmouth | OT |
| Norwich | NG | Bristol | OU |
| Northampton | NH | Birmingham | OV |
| Brighton | NJ | Portsmouth | OW |
| Luton | NK | Birmingham | OX |
| Newcastle | NL | London NW | OY |
| Luton | NM | | |
| Nottingham | NN | Guildford | PA |
| Chelmsford | NO | Guildford | PB |
| Worcester | NP | Guildford | PC |
| Leicester | NR | Guildford | PD |
| Glasgow | NS | Guildford | PE |
| Shrewsbury | NT | Guildford | PF |

| Place | Code | Place | Code |
|---|---|---|---|
| Guildford | PG | Bournemouth | RU |
| Guildford | PH | Portsmouth | RV |
| Guildford | PJ | Coventry | RW |
| Guildford | PK | Reading | RX |
| Guildford | PL | Leicester | RY |
| Guildford | PM | | |
| Brighton | PN | Aberdeen | SA |
| Portsmouth | PO | Oban | SB |
| Luton | PP | Edinburgh | SC |
| Bournemouth | PR | Ayr | SD |
| Lerwick | PS | Keith | SE |
| Durham | PT | Edinburgh | SF |
| Chelmsford | PU | Edinburgh | SG |
| Ipswich | PV | Selkirk | SH |
| Norwich | PW | Ayr | SJ |
| Portsmouth | PX | Wick | SK |
| Middlesbrough | PY | Dundee | SL |
| | | Dumfries | SM |
| Nottingham | RA | Dundee | SN |
| Nottingham | RB | Aberdeen | SO |
| Nottingham | RC | Dundee | SP |
| Reading | RD | Dundee | SR |
| Stoke-on-Trent | RE | Aberdeen | SS |
| Stoke-on-Trent | RF | Inverness | ST |
| Newcastle-upon-Tyne | RG | Glasgow | SU |
| Hull | RH | Spare Marks | SV |
| Manchester | RJ | Dumfries | SW |
| London NW | RK | Edinburgh | SX |
| Truro | RL | Spare Marks | SY |
| Carlisle | RM | | |
| Preston | RN | Exeter | TA |
| Luton | RO | Warrington | TB |
| Northampton | RP | Bristol | TC |
| Nottingham | RR | Bolton | TD |
| Aberdeen | RS | Bolton | TE |
| Ipswich | RT | Reading | TF |

| | | | |
|---|---|---|---|
| Cardiff | **TG** | London C | **UU** |
| Swansea | **TH** | London C | **UV** |
| Liverpool | **TJ** | London C | **UW** |
| Plymouth | **TK** | Shrewsbury | **UX** |
| Lincoln | **TL** | Worcester | **UY** |
| Luton | **TM** | | |
| Newcastle-upon-Tyne | **TN** | Cambridge | **VA** |
| Nottingham | **TO** | Canterbury | **VB** |
| Portsmouth | **TP** | Coventry | **VC** |
| Portsmouth | **TR** | Luton | **VD** |
| Dundee | **TS** | Cambridge | **VE** |
| Exeter | **TT** | Norwich | **VF** |
| Chester | **TU** | Norwich | **VG** |
| Nottingham | **TV** | Huddersfield | **VH** |
| Chelmsford | **TW** | Hereford | **VJ** |
| Cardiff | **TX** | Newcastle-upon-Tyne | **VK** |
| Newcastle | **TY** | Lincoln | **VL** |
| | | Manchester | **VM** |
| Leeds | **UA** | Middlesbrough | **VN** |
| Leeds | **UB** | Nottingham | **VO** |
| London C | **UC** | Birmingham | **VP** |
| Oxford | **UD** | Manchester | **VR** |
| Dudley | **UE** | Luton | **VS** |
| Brighton | **UF** | Stoke-on-Trent | **VT** |
| Leeds | **UG** | Manchester | **VU** |
| Cardiff | **UH** | Northampton | **VV** |
| Shrewsbury | **UJ** | Chelmsford | **VW** |
| Birmingham | **UK** | Chelmsford | **VX** |
| London C | **UL** | York | **VY** |
| Leeds | **UM** | | |
| Barnstaple | **UN** | Sheffield | **WA** |
| Barnstaple | **UO** | Sheffield | **WB** |
| Durham | **UP** | Chelmsford | **WC** |
| Luton | **UR** | Dudley | **WD** |
| Glasgow | **US** | Sheffield | **WE** |
| Leicester | **UT** | Sheffield | **WF** |

| | | | |
|---|---|---|---|
| Sheffield | **WG** | Spare Marks | **XU** |
| Bolton | **WH** | Spare Marks | **XV** |
| Sheffield | **WJ** | Spare Marks | **XW** |
| Coventry | **WK** | Spare Marks | **XX** |
| Oxford | **WL** | Spare Marks | **XY** |
| Liverpool | **WM** | | |
| Swansea | **WN** | Taunton | **YA** |
| Cardiff | **WO** | Taunton | **YB** |
| Worcester | **WP** | Taunton | **YC** |
| Leeds | **WR** | Taunton | **YD** |
| Bristol | **WS** | London C | **YE** |
| Leeds | **WT** | London C | **YF** |
| Leeds | **WU** | Leeds | **YG** |
| Brighton | **WV** | London C | **YH** |
| Leeds | **WW** | Brighton | **YJ** |
| Leeds | **WX** | London C | **YK** |
| Leeds | **WY** | London C | **YL** |
| | | London C | **YM** |
| Spare Marks | **XA** | London C | **YN** |
| Spare Marks | **XB** | London C | **YO** |
| Spare Marks | **XC** | London C | **YP** |
| Spare Marks | **XD** | London C | **YR** |
| Spare Marks | **XE** | Glasgow | **YS** |
| Spare Marks | **XF** | London C | **YT** |
| Spare Marks | **XG** | London C | **YU** |
| Spare Marks | **XH** | London C | **YV** |
| Spare Marks | **XJ** | London C | **YW** |
| Spare Marks | **XK** | London C | **YX** |
| Spare Marks | **XL** | London C | **YY** |
| Spare Marks | **XM** | | |
| Spare Marks | **XN** | Dublin | **Z** |
| Spare Marks | **XO** | Dublin | **ZA** |
| Spare Marks | **XP** | Cork | **ZB** |
| Spare Marks | **XR** | Dublin | **ZC** |
| Spare Marks | **XS** | Dublin | **ZD** |
| Spare Marks | **XT** | Dublin | **ZE** |

| | |
|---|---|
| Cork | **ZF** |
| Dublin | **ZH** |
| Dublin | **ZI** |
| Dublin | **ZJ** |
| Cork | **ZK** |
| Dublin | **ZL** |
| Galway | **ZM** |
| Meath | **ZN** |
| Dublin | **ZO** |
| Donegal | **ZP** |
| Wexford | **ZR** |
| Cork | **ZT** |
| Dublin | **ZU** |
| Kildare | **ZW** |
| Kerry | **ZX** |
| Louth | **ZY** |
| Dublin C.B.C. | **ZZ** |
| The Royal Irish Automobile Club, Dublin | **ZZ** |
| The Automobile Association, Dublin | **ZZ** |

# When was it registered

| Suffix | Year |
|---|---|
| A | 1963 |
| B | 1964 |
| C | 1965 |
| D | 1966 |
| E | January to July, 1967 |
| F | After 1st August, 1967 |
| G | After 1st August, 1968 |
| H | After 1st August, 1969 |
| J | After 1st August, 1970 |
| K | After 1st August, 1971 |
| L | After 1st August, 1972 |
| M | After 1st August, 1973 |
| N | After 1st August, 1974 |
| P | After 1st August, 1975 |
| R | After 1st August, 1976 |
| S | After 1st August, 1977 |
| T | After 1st August, 1978 |

# International registration plates

Vehicles are required to bear a plate indicating their country of origin when travelling in a foreign country. This plate usually consists of letters in black on a white background. See how many you can spot on the road. Attempts are being made to standardise these international registration letters so that they can be used for aircraft and boats, as well as cars. The letters given in brackets are the suggested new letters for each country.

(Where a country is marked with an asterisk the rule of the road is

'Drive on the Left'. For the unmarked countries the rule is 'Drive on the Right'.)

| | |
|---|---|
| A (AT) | Austria |
| ADN (YD) | Democratic Yemen (formerly Aden)* |
| AFG (AF) | Afghanistan |
| AL | Albania |
| AND (AD) | Andorra |
| AUS (AU) | Australia* |
| B (BE) | Belgium |
| BDS (BB) | Barbados* |
| BG | Bulgaria |
| BH (BZ) | Belize (formerly British Honduras) |
| BR | Brazil |
| BRN (BH) | Bahrain |
| BRU (BN) | Brunei* |
| BS | Bahamas* |
| BUR (BU) | Burma |
| C (CU) | Cuba |
| CDN (CA) | Canada |
| CH | Switzerland |
| CI | Ivory Coast |
| CL (LK) | Sri Lanka (formerly Ceylon)* |
| CO | Colombia |
| CR | Costa Rica |
| CS | Czechoslovakia |
| CY | Cyprus* |
| D (DE) | German Federal Republic |
| DDR (DD) | German Democratic Republic |
| DK | Denmark |
| DOM (DG) | Dominican Republic |
| DY | Dahomey |
| DZ | Algeria |
| E (ES) | Spain |
| EAK (KE) | Kenya* |
| EAT (TZ) | Tanzania (formerly Tanganika) |
| EAU (UG) | Uganda* |
| EAZ (TZ) | Tanzania (formerly Zanzibar)* |
| EC | Ecuador |
| ET (EG) | Arab Republic of Egypt |
| F (FR) | France |
| FJI (FJ) | Fiji* |
| FL (LI) | Liechtenstein |
| GB | United Kingdom of Great Britain and Northern Ireland* |
| GBA | Alderney* |
| GBG | Guernsey* |
| GBJ | Jersey* |
| GBM | Isle of Man* |
| GBZ (GI) | Gibraltar |
| GCA (GT) | Guatemala |
| GH | Ghana |
| GR | Greece |
| GUY (GY) | Guyana* |
| H (HU) | Hungary |
| HK | Hong Kong* |
| HKJ (JO) | Jordan |
| I (IT) | Italy |
| IL | Israel |
| IND (IN) | India* |
| IR | Iran |
| IRL (IE) | Ireland |
| IRQ (IQ) | Iraq |
| IS | Iceland |
| J (JP) | Japan* |
| JA (JM) | Jamaica* |
| K (KH) | Kampuchea (formerly Cambodia) |
| KWT (KW) | Kuwait |
| L (LU) | Luxembourg |
| LAO (LA) | Laos |

| | | | |
|---|---|---|---|
| LAR (LY) | Libya | RIM (MR) | Mauritania |
| LB (LR) | Liberia | RL (LB) | Lebanon |
| LS | Lesotho (formerly Basutoland)* | RM (MG) | Malagasy Republic (formerly Madagascar) |
| M (MT) | Malta* | | |
| MA | Morocco | RMM (ML) | Mali |
| MAL (MY) | Malaysia* | ROK (KP) | Korea (Republic of) |
| MB (MU) | Mauritius* | | |
| MC | Monaco | RP (PH) | Philippines |
| MEX (MX) | Mexico | RSM (SM) | San Marino |
| MW | Malawi* | RSR (RH) | Rhodesia (formerly Southern Rhodesia*) |
| N (NO) | Norway | | |
| NA (AN) | Netherlands Antilles | | |
| | | RU (BI) | Burundi |
| NIC (NI) | Nicaragua | RWA (RW) | Rwanda |
| NL | Netherlands | S (SE) | Sweden |
| NZ | New Zealand* | SD (SZ) | Swaziland* |
| P (AO) | Angola | SF (FI) | Finland |
| P (CV) | Cape Verde Islands | SGP (SG) | Singapore* |
| P (MZ) | Mozambique* | SME (SR) | Surinam |
| P (GN) | Guinea | SN | Senegal |
| P (PT) | Portugal | SU | Union of Soviet Socialist Republics |
| P (TP) | Timor | | |
| P (ST) | São Tomé and Principe | SWA | South West Africa* (Namibia) |
| PA | Panama | SY (SC) | Seychelles* |
| PAK (PK) | Pakistan* | SYR (SY) | Syria |
| PE | Peru | T (TH) | Thailand* |
| PL | Poland | TG | Togo |
| PY | Paraguay | TN | Tunisia |
| R (RO) | Romania | TR | Turkey |
| RA (AR) | Argentina | TT | Trinidad and Tobago* |
| RB (RW) | Botswana (formerly Bechuanaland)* | | |
| | | U (UY) | Uruguay |
| RC (TW) | Taiwan (Formosa) | USA (US) | United States of America |
| RCA (CF) | Central African Empire | | |
| | | V (VA) | Holy See (Vatican City) |
| RCB (CG) | Congo | | |
| RCH (CL) | Chile | VN (VD) | Vietnam (Republic of) |
| RH (HT) | Haiti | | |
| RI (ID) | Indonesia* | WAG (GM) | Gambia |

| WAL (SL) | Sierra Leone | WS | Western Samoa* |
|---|---|---|---|
| WAN (NG) | Nigeria | WV(VC) | St Vincent |
| WD (DM) | Dominica | | (Windward |
| | (Windward | | Islands)* |
| | Islands)* | YU | Yugoslavia |
| WG (GD) | Granada | YV (VE) | Venezuela |
| | (Windward | Z | Zambia |
| | Islands)* | ZA | South Africa* |
| WL (LC) | St Lucia | ZR (ZM) | Zaire (formerly |
| | (Windward | | Congo Kinshasha) |
| | Islands)* | | |

*Right:* Some signs displayed on goods vehicles. Shown top right is the 'Hazchem' vehicle marker. '2YE' indicates the action to be taken and the action to be avoided in the case of an accident. '1089' is the United Nations code number for the chemical, and below this is the 24-hour telephone number of the manufacturer.

## Signs on goods vehicles

### Inflammable loads

The flame symbol displayed at the front and rear of a vehicle indicates that its load is inflammable. You will usually find that the telephone number to contact in case of an emergency is also shown on the vehicle.

### Corrosive loads

The black and white symbol has to be displayed on vehicles carrying corrosive substances. To find out what substance the vehicle is carrying look on the side of the vehicle where the law states that the name of the substance must be displayed in red letters on a white background.

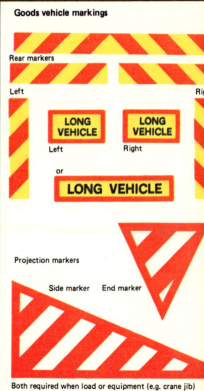

Goods vehicle markings

Rear markers

Left ... Rig

LONG VEHICLE  LONG VEHICLE

Left  Right

or

LONG VEHICLE

Projection markers

Side marker   End marker

Both required when load or equipment (e.g. crane jib) overhangs front or rear by more than 1.83 metres.

## Radioactive loads

A vehicle bearing the symbol each side is carrying radioactive material. The symbol is either black on an orange background as shown, or may consist of black lettering on a white diamond.

## Other dangerous loads

On some vehicles carrying dangerous loads you will see a sign as shown here. It is called a 'Hazchem Vehicle Marker' and it enables a fireman to identify the nature of the hazardous load, and what action to take in an emergency. The Hazchem code was prepared by the London Fire Brigade and the code number is displayed on the label, as is a United Nations code number. Firemen carry a pocket reference card which tells them whether they need to wear protective clothing, or breathing apparatus, and how they should tackle the emergency.

## Long and heavy vehicles

Commercial vehicles that weigh more than 3 tonnes unladen, and trailers weighing over 1 tonne unladen must bear, at the rear of the vehicle, reflective markers consisting of fluorescent red and yellow diagonal stripes as shown here.

If a vehicle is more than 13 metres (42·6 feet) in length it must show the 'Long Vehicle' sign in addition to the normal reflective markers. A number of vehicles are, however, exempt from this regulation. Broken-down vehicles being towed, fire engines, car carriers, and vehicles owned by the armed forces are just some that are not required by law to display the notice, although there is nothing to stop them from doing so if they wish. Special triangles have to be displayed on the side and rear of a vehicle when its load extends beyond the ends of the vehicle. This applies when the load extends more than 1·83 metres (6 feet) beyond the front or the rear of the vehicle. If the load extends more than 1·07 metres (3·5

The panel illustrated is for an inflammable liquid. Diamond symbols indicating other risks include:

Compressed gases

Poisonous substances

Oxidizing substances

Corrosive substances

Substances liable to ignite spontaneously

Radioactive substances

feet) beyond the rear of the vehicle it is still necessary to draw attention to the fact and a piece of rag tied to the end of the load is usually used for this purpose.

The law also sets down rules regarding the provision of additional lights on long loads. Additional rearlights have to be carried if the load extends for more than 1·07 metres (3·5 feet) beyond the vehicle's own lights, or if its lights are obscured by the load.

### TIR

On some goods vehicles you will see a large sign bearing the letters TIR. These stand for *Touring Internationale Routier*. The purpose of this system is to enable vehicles to carry goods from country to country with the minimum of customs formalities. Customs officers seal the load at the port of embarkation and it must then remain sealed until it reaches its final destination. This means the driver need not have his load examined every time he crosses a frontier and saves a lot of time and unnecessary frustration.

It is still possible to transport goods abroad without a TIR permit, but in this case the driver has to comply with the individual customs requirements of each country through which he travels.

## Number plates of the armed forces

All vehicles of the armed forces have different number plates from civilian cars and lorries. There is no general rule to identify either the type or the age of the vehicle. The number plates consist of two numbers, two letters and then two numbers, e.g. 24 CL 48.

All Royal Air Force vehicles use the letter A first. All Royal Navy vehicles use the letters RN. All other letters will be for Army vehicles. The latest Army vehicles will probably have numbers in the F and G letter sequences.

## Rank plates of the armed forces

High-ranking officers of the Army, Royal Navy and Royal Air Force have special plates on their vehicles bearing silver stars. The number of stars indicates the owner's rank as shown below:

|  | Army | Royal Navy | Royal Air Force |
|---|---|---|---|
| * | Brigadier | Commodore 1st class | Air Commodore |
| ** | Major General | Rear Admiral | Air Vice Marshal |
| *** | Lieutenant General | Vice Admiral | Air Marshal |
| **** | General | Admiral | Air Chief Marshal |
| ***** | Field Marshal | Admiral of the Fleet | Marshal of the RAF |

The background colour of the plate will tell you which of the three forces it represents:

*Army plates are red*
*Royal Navy plates are dark blue*
*Royal Air Force plates are light blue*

Vehicles of defence staff and senior officers of the Ministry of Defence also bear similar plates. These are striped, with a dark blue band at the top, a red band in the middle and a light blue band at the bottom.

## CD plates

The letters CD stand for *Corps Diplomatique*. Such a plate on a vehicle usually means that it belongs to an embassy or a consulate.

## Institute of Advanced Motorists

The triangular IAM symbol is seen on the cars of drivers who have passed the *advanced* driving test. The standard, compulsory driving test is nothing more than a simple examination of the driver's basic skills, and as such is no proof that the candidate is a good driver. Most drivers realise that passing the driving test is only the start of their motoring career. Good drivers are anxious to improve their motoring skills and require some means of assessing their ability. The advanced test, organised by The Institute of Advanced Motorists, is designed to do this with the objective of making

roads safer by raising the general standard of driving.

The Institute, founded in 1956, is a non-profit-making organisation. The test lasts about an hour and a half and covers a route of between 56 and 64 kilometers (35 and 40 miles) incorporating road conditions of all kinds. Since its inauguration some 200,000 drivers have taken the test and about 60 per cent have passed.

## Goods carried by road transport in Great Britain

| | Percentage |
|---|---|
| Cereals | 2 |
| Fresh fruit and vegetables | 3 |
| Other food, drink and tobacco | 16 |
| Vegetable oils and fats | 1 |
| Timber | 2 |
| Fertilizer | 1 |
| Crude minerals, sand, gravel and ores | 24 |
| Solid fuels | 7 |
| Petrol and petroleum products | 5 |
| Tar | 1 |
| Chemicals | 2 |
| Lime, cement and building materials | 18 |
| Metals | 4 |
| Metal manufactures | 2 |
| Machinery | 2 |
| Miscellaneous manufactured articles | 6 |
| Other goods | 4 |

# Index *Numbers in bold refer to illustrations.*